DESIGNING ENGINEERING SOLUTIONS

Inventors of Health and Medical Technology

Heather S. Morrison

New York

Published in 2016 by Cavendish Square Publishing, LLC
243 5th Avenue, Suite 136, New York, NY 10016

Copyright © 2016 by Cavendish Square Publishing, LLC

First Edition

No part of this publication may be reproduced, stored in a retrieval system, or transmitted in any form or by any means—electronic, mechanical, photocopying, recording, or otherwise—without the prior permission of the copyright owner. Request for permission should be addressed to Permissions, Cavendish Square Publishing, 243 5th Avenue, Suite 136, New York, NY 10016. Tel (877) 980-4450; fax (877) 980-4454.

Website: cavendishsq.com

This publication represents the opinions and views of the author based on his or her personal experience, knowledge, and research. The information in this book serves as a general guide only. The author and publisher have used their best efforts in preparing this book and disclaim liability rising directly or indirectly from the use and application of this book.

CPSIA Compliance Information: Batch #WS15CSQ

All websites were available and accurate when this book was sent to press.

Library of Congress Cataloging-in-Publication Data

Morrison, Heather S., author.
Inventors of health and medical technology / Heather S. Morrison.
pages cm. — (Designing engineering solutions)
Includes bibliographical references and index.
ISBN 978-1-50260-658-7 (hardcover) ISBN 978-1-50260-659-4 (ebook)
1. Medical technology—Biography—Juvenile literature. 2. Medical technology—History—Juvenile literature.
3. Medicine—Biography—Juvenile literature. 4. Medicine—History—Juvenile literature.
5. Inventors—Biography—Juvenile literature. I. Title.

R855.4.M67 2016
610.92—dc23

2014049162

The author would like to thank the following contributors: Laura Lambert, Paul Schellinger, Mary Sisson, Cathleen Small, Gwendolyn Wells, Chris Woodford

Editorial Director: David McNamara
Editor: Kristen Susienka
Copy Editor: Michele Suchomel-Casey
Art Director: Jeffrey Talbot
Designer: Alan Sliwinski
Senior Production Manager: Jennifer Ryder-Talbot
Production Editor: Renni Johnson
Photo Research: J8 Media

The photographs in this book are used by permission and through the courtesy of: Morgan Hank/Science Source/Getty Images, cover and frontispiece; Ang Intaravichian/Shutterstock.com, 4; Shane Maritch/Shutterstock.com, 6; RNL Bio Co. Ltd. via Getty Images, 11; Science Photo Library/Getty Images, 15; National Library of Medicine/File: Patricia Bath.jpg/Wikimedia Commons, 16; Bork/Shutterstock.com, 18; Courtesy USPTO, 20; Wellcome Library, London/File: World War II; wounded soldiers convalescing at Preston Hall Wellcome L0074417.jpg/Wikimedia Commons, 21; Keystone-France/Gamma-Keystone via Getty Images, 23; iStockphoto.com/No beast so fierce, 25; Jane Gitschier/File:Herbert Boyer.png/Wikimedia Commons, Ted Streshinsky/The LIFE Images Collection/Getty Images, 26; David M. Phillips/Science Source/Getty Images, 29; Handout/Getty Images, 33; Mike Clarke/AFP/Getty Images, 35; Volker Steger/Science Source, 39; Science & Society Picture Library/Getty Images, 41; Central Press/Hulton Archive/Getty Images, AIP Emilio Segre Visual Archives, Physics Today Collection, 42; Keystone/Hulton Archive/Getty Images, 47; Manuel Litran/Paris Match via Getty Images, 49; Courtesy Fonar Corporation, 50; AIP Emilio Segre Visual Archives, 54; Nyvlt-art/Shutterstock.com, 56; Alfred Eisenstaedt/The LIFE Picture Collection/Getty Images, 57; Private Collection/DaTo Images/Bridgeman Images, 61; Victor Habbick Visions/Science Photo Library/Getty Images, 63; Central Press/Getty Images, 64; Keystone/Getty Images 69; Tarasyuk Igor/Shutterstock.com, 71; Courtesy Steve Adams/Lawrence Berkeley National Laboratory © 2010 The Regents of the University of California, Lawrence Berkeley National Laboratory, 72; Roy Kaltschmidt/Berkeley Lab © 2013 The Regents of the University of California, Lawrence Berkeley National Laboratory, 74; Voisin/Phanie/SuperStock, 76; AP Photo, 77; AP Photo, 78; Jeannot Olivet/E+/Getty Images, 83; AP Photo/Bill Sikes, File, 84; Yale Joel/The LIFE Picture Collection/Getty Images, 87; Science & Society Picture Library/Getty Images, 91; Private Collection/Look and Learn/Bridgeman Images, 92; Hulton Archive/Getty Images, 95; Wellcome Library, London/File: A patient in bed with smallpox, attended by a physician. Col Wellcome L0030552.jpg/Wikimedia Commons, 97; John Raphael Smith/(Public Domain) File: Edward Jenner.jpg/Wikimedia Commons, 98; By Yann Forget/File: World Health Organisation building south face 2.jpg - Wikimedia Commons, 103; BSIP/Universal Images Group/Getty Images, 105; AP Photo, 106; Francis Miller/The LIFE Picture Collection/Getty Images, 110; Evikka/Shutterstock.com, 112; Paul Morigi/Getty Images for The Friars Club, 113; Chris Fitzgerald/Candidate Photos/Newscom, 115; Ernest Board (Public Domain) File:Morton Ether 1846.jpg/Wikimedia Commons, 120; Wellcome Library, London/ File:Portrait of William T. G. Morton. Wellcome M0002620.jpg /Wikimedia Commons, 121; Valentyn Volkov/Shutterstock.com, 126; AIP Emilio Segre Visual Archives, 127; Science Photo/Shutterstock.com, 132.

Printed in the United States of America

Contents

Introduction to Health and Medical Technology . . . 4

Patricia Bath
Inventor of Laser Cataract Surgery 15

Bessie Blount
Inventor of the Self-Feeding Apparatus for the Disabled . . 20

Herbert Boyer and Stanley Norman Cohen
Inventors of DNA Cloning . . . 25

Keith Campbell and Ian Wilmut
Inventors of Cloning Technology 33

Allan Cormack and Godfrey Hounsfield
Inventors of the CT Scanner 41

Raymond Damadian
Inventor of the Magnetic Resonance Imaging Scanner . . 49

Charles Drew
Creator of the Blood Bank . . . 56

Robert Edwards and Patrick Steptoe
Inventors of Human In Vitro Fertilization 63

Ashok Gadgil
Inventor of the Ultraviolet Water Purification System . . 71

Meredith Gourdine
Inventor of a Device for Purifying the Air 76

Wilson Greatbatch
Inventor of the Pacemaker . . 83

Robert Hooke
Inventor of Various Scientific Instruments 91

Edward Jenner
Inventor of the Smallpox Vaccine 97

Percy Lavon Julian
Inventor of the Glaucoma Treatment Method 105

Dean Kamen
Inventor of the AutoSyringe, the iBOT, and the Segway . . 112

William Morton
Pioneer in Anesthesia Device 120

Louis Pasteur
Inventor of Pasteurization . . 126

Glossary 135

Further Information 137

Index 143

Introduction to Health and Medical Technology

Throughout the centuries, humanity has advanced and thrived largely due to the inventions people have made. Perhaps one of the areas that has most benefited from new technologies has been the medical industry. Inventors have discovered new ways to help individuals throughout the centuries. Each new invention has improved lives around the world and has significantly enhanced the way the medical field operates. Key inventions over the years have included thermometers, stethoscopes, X-rays, vaccinations, pharmaceuticals, and cloning. Today, many other inventions are being made and becoming known in the medical industry. Each further improves our lifestyles and longevity, aiding people around the world.

The Origins of Medicine

Scientific and technical knowledge have increased systematically since ancient times, but medical knowledge has often lagged behind. In all parts of the world, early attempts to cure illnesses were based on folklore and religious beliefs. For centuries, natural plants such as herbs, selected by trial and error, were used to treat wounds and ailments. As time went on, however, other techniques were used.

The ancient Greeks, who developed some of the earliest scientific ideas, also made some of the first real attempts to determine the underlying causes of illness and disease. Sometimes known as the father of medicine, Greek philosopher Hippocrates (circa 460–375 BCE) refused to accept that diseases were punishments sent by the gods, as people had once thought. Thinking like a scientist, he wrote, "Every disease has its own nature, and arises from external causes." Galen of Pergamum (ca. 129–216 CE) was another pioneering doctor of ancient times. By dissecting the bodies of apes, he helped to found the sciences of anatomy, which explores the major structures inside the body, and physiology, which considers the more detailed inner workings of these structures. The ideas propounded by the ancients proved hugely influential. Galen's work was used for centuries, while Hippocrates gave his name to the Hippocratic oath, a pledge to put the interests of patients first. This code of medical ethics remains as a guide for physicians today.

Advancing the Medical Industry

Medicine advanced to a more scientific footing during the Renaissance, around the fifteenth century, when science began to challenge religion as the most accurate explanation of human experience. In the 1490s, the famous Italian artist and inventor Leonardo da Vinci (1452–1519) made sketches of the body's inner workings in his notebooks. About fifty years later, Flemish physician Andreas Vesalius (1514–1564) published the first reliable textbook of detailed drawings showing the inner structures of the human body.

Scientific inventions helped medicine greatly. During the seventeenth century, English scientist Robert Hooke (1635–1703) developed the modern **compound microscope**, which made the study of organisms otherwise invisible to the naked eye possible. Using his invention, he observed the tiny "building blocks" from which living things were made and became the first person to call them cells. Used to study cadavers, microscopes greatly expanded the sciences of

Inventing Drugs

Drugs are among the oldest medical inventions. In India, ancient physicians used hundreds of different medicines made from animal substances such as milk and bone, as well as from vegetables and minerals. The ancient Chinese developed a similar system based on herbal remedies that is still widely used. Some ancient remedies are still used in Western medicine. Aspirin, one of the world's most popular drugs, is made from a chemical found in the bark of the willow tree, which was known to ancient Greeks and Native Americans as a painkiller. It was first made as a drug in 1897 by German chemist Felix Hoffmann (1868–1946) to help relieve his father's arthritis.

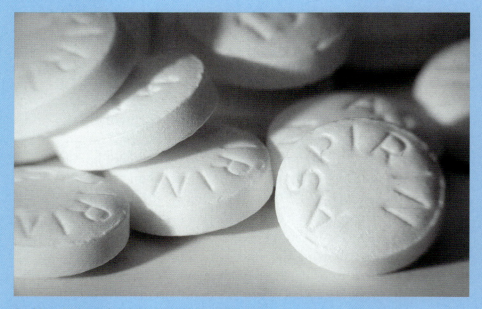

Aspirin originates from the bark of the willow tree.

anatomy and physiology. For example, later medical scientists, such as the German Rudolf Virchow (1821–1902), built on Hooke's work, showing how living cells could make healthy tissue grow but, at the same time, were at the center of illness and disease.

About fifty years later, German physicist Daniel Fahrenheit (1686–1736) invented the first practical thermometers and the

> The antibiotic penicillin, discovered by Alexander Fleming (1881–1955) in 1928, proved to be a revolutionary drug treatment for many illnesses caused by germs. Another modern drug pioneer was American chemist Percy Lavon Julian (1899–1975). Early in his career he invented physostigmine, a drug that could successfully treat **glaucoma**, an eye disease. Thousands of other drugs are now in use worldwide. They include antiseptics (to kill bacteria), anesthetics (for dulling pain), cytotoxic drugs (for killing cancer cells), and anti-inflammatory drugs (which can relieve the swollen, painful joints of arthritis).
>
> During the twentieth century, drugs became an especially important treatment for mental illnesses. In the early 1950s, Czech-born chemist Frank Berger (1913–2008) discovered chemicals that could calm angry monkeys—and thus invented the first human tranquilizer drugs, Miltown and Equanil. Shortly afterward, chemist Leo Sternbach (1908–2005), working for the Roche company, developed tranquilizers with fewer side effects. In the following decade, Ray Fuller (1935–1996) and his team at the Eli Lilly Company began selling fluoxetine, a drug that proved to be an effective treatment for depression. Commonly known as Prozac, it became the most popular psychiatric drug in history within three years of its launch.
>
> Apart from bringing real benefits to health, effective drugs can tell medical scientists a great deal about how the body works. For example, scientists know that Prozac affects the way the chemical serotonin is absorbed by the brain. Since Prozac can relieve depression, its effectiveness has helped to confirm that serotonin is involved in depressive illnesses. Successful drugs therefore play an important part in increasing medical knowledge.

Fahrenheit temperature scale. This discovery enabled physicians to monitor people's health by measuring how hot or cold their bodies were. Another great medical invention came about a century later, in 1819, when French physician René Laënnec (1781–1826) invented the **stethoscope**. The thermometer and stethoscope gave physicians a better idea of what might be happening inside someone's body. They proved to be great aids to diagnosis, which is the first step to successful treatment.

Protecting Against Illness

One of the greatest medical advances of the eighteenth century came from an inspired discovery made by English physician Edward Jenner (1749–1823). At that time, many people were dying from smallpox. Jenner noticed that people suffering from another disease—**cowpox**—did not get smallpox. This led him to invent **vaccination**. Jenner also studied the causes of smallpox and was the first to use the word "virus" to explain how the disease was transmitted.

At the time the causes of disease were hotly debated. Some physicians believed in an old theory—spontaneous generation—that claimed diseases could arise from inanimate objects. About a half-century after Jenner's breakthrough, Louis Pasteur (1822–1895), a French scientist, proved that diseases are actually spread by bacteria and viruses; this idea became known as the germ theory of disease. Using this theory, Pasteur developed important vaccines for diseases such as anthrax, cholera, and rabies. His scientific breakthrough also enabled him to invent **pasteurization**.

Pasteur's work began the science of bacteriology, which was in turn advanced by others. A Scottish surgeon, Joseph Lister (1827–1912), realized that germs in the operating room greatly endangered the lives of his patients. When he started spraying the operating theater with the antiseptic (germ-killing) carbolic acid before operations, many more of his patients survived. In the 1880s, German physician Robert Koch (1843–1910) took Pasteur's work in a different direction, using microscopes to identify the bacteria that caused diseases such as tuberculosis and cholera.

Another important breakthrough in the fight against disease came in 1928, when the English bacteriologist Alexander Fleming accidentally invented penicillin. Fleming found that a mold growing in a dish in his laboratory was very effective at killing bacteria. Later, the mold (*Penicillium notatum*) was used to make the antibiotic drug penicillin. Many other antibiotics have been developed since then.

Surgery Improves

Doctors have used surgery since ancient times. Until the nineteenth century, however, surgery was often agonizing because patients were usually awake throughout their operation. A great development in surgery came in 1846 when the American dentist William Morton (1819–1868) invented general anesthetic, a way of using a gas to render the patient unconscious; thus the patient did not feel the pain of surgery. Almost exactly a century later, American physician Charles Drew (1904–1950) made another great surgical advancement when he set up the world's first large-scale blood bank.

Advances such as these made possible ever more ambitious—and contentious—operations. One of the most controversial forms of surgery yet attempted was pioneered in 1967 when a South African doctor, Christiaan Barnard (1922–2001), carried out the world's first heart transplant. Such dramatic operations carry a high risk of failure and are immensely traumatic for patients; however, if successful, they can prolong the recipient's life.

Minor operations are now often carried out in a less intrusive way using the keyhole surgery technique; a small incision is made in a patient's body, and the procedure is done without making large incisions. Lasers are also used in modern operations because they can cut soft tissue very precisely. They were invented in the 1950s by American physicists Arthur Schawlow (1921–1999) and Charles Townes (1915–2015). Lasers have been widely used in eye surgery since the 1980s, when African American physician Patricia Bath (1942–) pioneered their use for removing cataracts, a cloudiness in the lens of the eye that can cause blindness.

Atoms in Medicine

The most dramatic scientific and technological advances of the twentieth century came about with the discovery of the world inside atoms, the tiny particles from which all substances are made. More effective medical diagnosis and treatment were among the more positive developments of atomic technology. X-rays (powerful, invisible electromagnetic waves) were accidentally discovered in 1895 by German physicist Wilhelm Röntgen (1845–1923) and have been used by physicians ever since to study such things as broken bones.

In the 1970s, British scientists Allan Cormack (1924–1998) and Godfrey Hounsfield (1919–2004) developed a type of improved X-ray machine, known as computerized axial tomography (CAT or CT). As its name suggests, it uses a computer to make detailed, three-dimensional images of the body by scanning X-ray beams through it. Medical techniques like this have revolutionized diagnosis, especially in the field of neuroscience. Another revolutionary form of scanning, known as magnetic resonance imaging (MRI), was developed in the 1970s and 1980s by biological physicist Raymond Damadian (1936–). Unlike X-rays, which show hard substances like bones and teeth, an MRI builds a picture of the soft tissues in the body and is better for locating problems such as tumors.

Atomic technology has proved equally useful in treating some of the illnesses it has helped to diagnose. One year after Röntgen chanced upon X-rays, French physicist Antoine-Henri Becquerel (1852–1908) discovered **radioactivity**. Another pioneer in this area, Polish-born physicist and chemist Marie Curie (1867–1934), used her knowledge to discover a new chemical element, called radium, in 1898. Soon afterward, radium was used to develop the first radiation treatments for cancer—the disease that, tragically, claimed Curie's own life.

Moving into the Modern Age

Even before the advent of modern medicine, physicians had observed that certain illnesses tended to run in families. Since the mid-twentieth century, a new science—genetics—has given doctors an entirely new insight into inherited disease. The genetics age began in 1953 when English physicist Francis Crick (1916–2004) and American biologist James Watson (1928–) discovered the structure of the chemical deoxyribonucleic acid (DNA). DNA is contained in every living cell and carries the genetic information that works like a set of instructions to tell the cell how to develop.

Since the discovery of DNA, biologists have believed that DNA also contained the secrets of many illnesses because it could instruct cells to malfunction. By studying DNA, scientists hoped to discover how to stop certain illnesses from developing or prevent them from being passed from parents to children. Before scientists could begin to do so, however, they had to discover the meaning of the body's entire set of genetic information, which is known as the human genome. An ambitious thirteen-year worldwide effort, the Human Genome Project,

Two cloned beagles are shown at National Seoul University in 2009.

had successfully mapped all of the information in human DNA (equivalent to two hundred volumes of a typical telephone directory) by 2003. Recently, scientists have used this information to better understand hereditary diseases, and some predict DNA sequencing could become entirely affordable by 2020, enabling more advances in medicine and treatments.

Materials That Aided Medicine

One of the biggest areas of technological advances of the twentieth century was the development of artificial (synthetic) materials, which have revolutionized everything from clothing design to aerospace. Medicine has also benefited enormously from these new materials. For example, nylon, the revolutionary synthetic fiber invented in the 1930s by American chemist Wallace Carothers (1896–1937), is one of the materials used to stitch wounds together.

Since the 1970s, surgeons have been replacing worn-out body parts with bionic (artificially engineered) replacements made from such materials as silicone, rubber, plastics, and carbon fibers. One of the best-known examples is used in hip replacement surgery. In place of worn-out bone joints, many older people—especially those suffering from arthritis—now have artificial hip joints made from metal balls that rotate smoothly in plastic sockets. The latest artificial limbs (prosthetics) are also made from high-tech materials such as carbon fibers.

Another important treatment involves growing new tissues in the laboratory, then using them to repair damaged or diseased parts of the body. If a person suffers skin damage, perhaps in a fire, a small sample of existing skin, the size of a postage stamp, can be used to grow a large area of replacement skin (skin graft) in just a few weeks.

A related treatment involves using fetal tissue to replace or regenerate damaged tissue in a patient's body or brain. For example, doctors have managed to relieve the symptoms of Parkinson's disease by injecting fetal cells into the basal ganglia—a part of the brain. Although the treatment is effective, it has been very controversial and raises ethical issues about the uses of human embryos.

The process of manipulating genetic information is called genetic engineering. Removing all or part of an organism's DNA and transferring it into another organism in which it can grow are a means of exactly copying living cells. This technique, called cloning, was developed in the early 1970s by Herbert Boyer (1936–) and Stanley Cohen (1935–). Its first use was in manufacturing the drug insulin, a treatment for diabetes. Since, it has been successfully used in sheep as well as in human embryos, and it may one day be used to regrow human body parts, or even entire human beings.

Modern Medicine

Great improvements to people's lives are often achieved through simple inventions. One example has been the development of fiber optics: a way of transmitting light down flexible glass pipes that has revolutionized telecommunications. The idea was originally developed in the 1950s by Indian physicist Narinder Kapany (1926–). Later in that decade, American scientists used fiber optics to build the first gastroscope, a medical device that could help doctors see inside people's stomachs by looking through a flexible glass tube inserted down a patient's throat.

In vitro fertilization (IVF) is another simple invention that has made a huge difference to many people who have been unable to conceive children naturally. IVF involves removing eggs from a woman's ovaries and fertilizing them with a man's sperm in a laboratory dish. The fertilized eggs are then returned to the woman's womb, where they develop normally. The technique was pioneered by two British doctors, Patrick Steptoe (1913–1988) and Robert Edwards (1925–2013), who helped to produce the first IVF baby, Louise Brown, in July 1978. In 2012, researchers estimated that more than five million babies worldwide had been born by IVF.

Many inventors have made a difference to the lives of the disabled. An invention developed by American Bessie Blount (1914–2009) greatly improved the lives of people who had lost the ability to feed themselves. Blount's idea was an electrically controlled feeding tube that could deliver portions of food automatically whenever the disabled person bit into it. Another American inventor, Dean Kamen

(1951–), is perhaps best known for developing an electrically powered, two-wheeled trolley—the Segway personal transporter. However, he has also made inventions for the disabled, including the revolutionary iBOT wheelchair. With four-wheel drive and a built-in gyroscope (a heavy, rapidly spinning wheel) to aid in balance, the iBOT can negotiate rough terrain, lift itself up to standing height, and even climb stairs. Kamen's other inventions include a mobile dialysis machine, an automatic device for giving insulin injections to people with diabetes, and an engine that can purify water for developing countries.

Lack of clean water is one of the biggest causes of illness in the developing world. Figures published in 2013 by the World Health Organization show that, worldwide, 2.5 billion people lack basic water facilities and many do not have proper sanitation. As a result, an estimated 1.5 million children die each year from illnesses such as diarrhea, cholera, and hepatitis, which can be carried in dirty water. Kamen is not the only inventor to try to tackle this problem. In 1993, Indian-born American scientist Ashok Gadgil (1950–) began developing a simple invention that could disinfect a ton (0.9 metric tons) of water for just half a cent. Using ultraviolet light and powered by a simple car battery, it can kill 99.999 percent of bacteria and produce enough clean water for one thousand people.

Over the centuries, medical inventions have saved many millions of people's lives. Many inventions, such as vaccines, penicillin, and blood banks, have greatly increased people's life expectancy. Others, such as microscopes, X-rays, and medical scanners, have helped scientists better understand diseases and other illnesses, as well as improve measures used against them. As the world progresses and further advancements are made, new technologies will benefit humanity, leading to a safer, healthier population.

Inventor of Laser Cataract Surgery

Patricia Bath

1942–

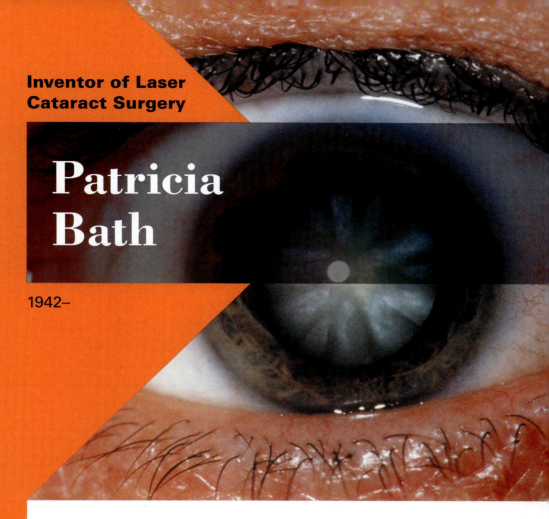

Over the years, as medical advancements have improved conditions for patients around the world, several inventors have created techniques that have benefited people with disabilities. Patricia Bath wanted to help people who could not see clearly due to cataracts, a condition that, without treatment, can cause blindness. Her invention, a new method of laser surgery presented in the 1980s, transformed the eye-medicine field and preserved millions of people's sight. It also earned her the first patent for a medical device ever granted to a black woman doctor. Today, doctors commonly practice cataract surgery around the world.

Beginnings

Patricia Bath helped change the face of medicine.

Patricia Bath was born in 1942 and grew up in Harlem, a predominantly black neighborhood in New York City. Her father, an immigrant from the Caribbean island of Trinidad, worked as a merchant seaman; he subsequently became the first black motorman to work in the New York City subway system. Her mother worked as a housekeeper; Bath recalls, "She scrubbed floors so that I could go to medical school."

Bath had an early interest in science and medicine, taking inspiration from the life of Albert Schweitzer, who won a **Nobel Prize** in 1952 for his work with lepers in Africa. In high school, she excelled in science, winning various awards.

In 1959, she was selected to be part of a summer program sponsored by the National Science Foundation. As part of the program, Bath, just sixteen years old, took part in advanced research on cancer. Her contributions were included in a scientific paper presented to an international group of scientists in September 1960. That year, Bath was one of ten US women to win the Mademoiselle Magazine Merit Award.

Having completed high school in just two and a half years, Bath enrolled in New York City's Hunter College, where she studied physics and chemistry. She then attended the Howard University School of Medicine in Washington, DC, becoming president of the Student National Medical Association. She graduated from Howard with honors in 1968 and returned to New York City to complete her training in ophthalmology.

Defining the Problem

During her training at two different New York City eye clinics—one at Harlem Hospital and one at Columbia University—Bath became acutely aware of the racial and economic disparities that existed in the field of eye care. Blindness among patients at Harlem Hospital, where the population was primarily black, was nearly twice as common as it was among patients at Columbia University.

Bath looked into the disparities and found that black communities had a general lack of access to eye care. From that point, she dedicated her life to providing eye care to underserved communities. She would later found, along with several colleagues, the American Institute for the Prevention of Blindness (AIPB). The AIPB worked to bring eye care to all communities, regardless of socioeconomic status, with the guiding principle that vision is a basic human right.

In 1970, Bath finished her training at New York University, where she was the first black resident in ophthalmology. Five years later, she moved to California to join the ophthalmology team at the University of California, Los Angeles (UCLA) Medical Center, where she became the first black woman surgeon on staff. She was also the first woman on staff at UCLA's Jules Stein Eye Institute.

Her trailblazing work did not end there. In 1983, she became the first woman in the United States to head a postgraduate training program in ophthalmology. Upon retirement, she would become the first woman elected to the honorary staff of the UCLA Medical Center. However, despite these landmark achievements, Bath is best known for pioneering work in eye surgery.

Designing the Solution

While at UCLA in the early 1980s, Bath began to think of a new way to treat cataracts. A cataract occurs when the lens of the eye, which is behind the iris and the pupil, becomes cloudy. Cataracts occur naturally over time, and they are especially common in men and women over sixty. They lead to blurry, distorted vision, and, if left untreated, blindness.

Traditionally, cataracts were removed using a drill-like device to grind the lens. This method was sometimes inexact and could cause harm to the eye. Bath believed that there was another way. She believed lasers could make the surgery faster, easier, more accurate, and less invasive.

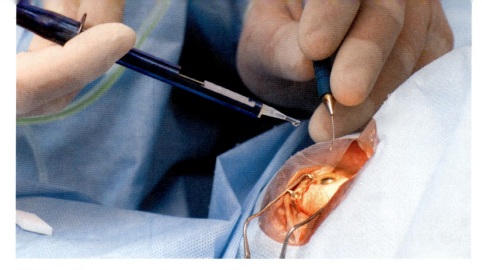

Doctors perform cataract surgery on a patient.

While laser technology has become a common part of medicine in contemporary times, in the early 1980s Bath had difficulty finding the tools to test her idea. She later recalled, "When I talked to people about it, they said it couldn't be done." Nearly five years and several trips to Berlin, Germany—home to some of the most advanced lasers at the time—were needed to accomplish the research and testing necessary to apply for a patent on the equipment Bath had designed.

Applying the Solution

By 1986, the technology was ready. Two years later, on May 17, 1988, Bath was awarded US Patent No. 47,444,360, for an "apparatus for ablating and removing cataract lenses." Bath's invention was a combination of a laser that, when inserted into the eye, would more or less vaporize the cataract, plus an irrigation system and suction tubes to remove the destroyed lens material. A new lens would then be inserted into the eye. The process was quick and virtually painless. Bath's invention would become known as the Laserphaco Probe. It is a process that preserved the sight of many people around the world and continues to this day.

Bath continued her work over the next decade and was granted several additional patents in the field of ophthalmology, including one, issued in 2000, for a method of cataract surgery involving ultrasound. She holds patents all over the world.

The Impact of the Solution on Society

Helping the blind to see was considered a miracle in biblical times. For Bath, it is her lifework. For more than thirty years, her inventions and her tireless dedication to securing the "right to sight" for people all over the world have restored vision to those who have been blind.

Bath has been honored repeatedly for her work. She was elected to the Hunter College Hall of Fame in 1988 and was honored as a Howard University Pioneer in Academic Medicine in 1993. In 2004, she was dubbed one of "California's Remarkable Women" as part of an exhibit at the California State History Museum. Although she has retired, Bath continues to work toward helping prevent, treat, and cure blindness for people the world over. The American Institute for the Prevention of Blindness still exists today, helping people in need. Bath has also become an advocate for **telemedicine**. With her influence, and the influence of others, the world's medical industry can work toward improving the lives of many more individuals.

Timeline

1942
Patricia Bath born in New York City

1959
While in high school, Bath participates in cancer research

1968
Bath graduates from Howard University School of Medicine

1970
Bath completes her ophthalmology training

1986
Bath completes research and testing for a procedure to remove cataracts using lasers

1988
Bath receives a patent for the Laserphaco Probe

2000
Bath receives a patent for a method of cataract surgery involving ultrasound

Inventor of Self-Feeding Apparatus for the Disabled

Bessie Blount

1914–2009

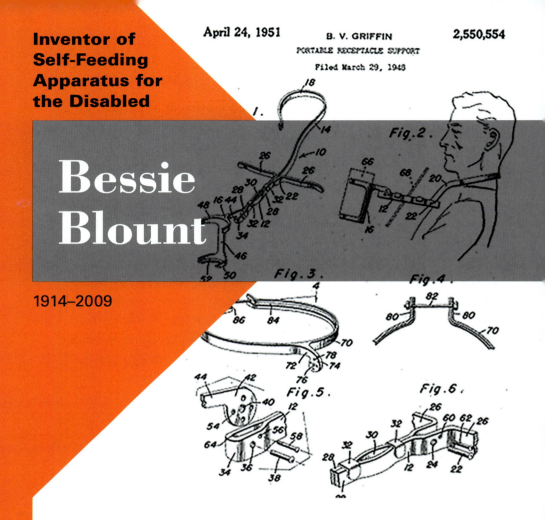

Prior to World War II, many people suffering from wounds on the battlefield struggled to eat. Men who lost arms or hands were especially vulnerable, since they could not maneuver their bodies as they once had done. Once war broke out in the 1940s, however, there entered a new hope with an African American woman named Bessie Blount. She was a **physical therapist** who cared for wounded soldiers. Her invention, of a self-feeding apparatus, allowed men to feed themselves without needing their arms or hands. This revolutionized medicine and the way soldiers, and other people who were disabled, viewed themselves once they reentered civilian life.

Unknown Origins

Bessie Blount was born November 24, 1914, in Hickory, Virginia. Little is known about her childhood, apart from the fact that she grew up wanting to pursue a medical career. As a young woman she left Virginia to attend the Panzer College of Physical Education (later part of Montclair State University) in East Orange, New Jersey. She also trained as a physical therapist at Union Junior College in New Jersey and at facilities in Chicago.

Defining the Problem

While working as a physical therapist at various veterans' hospitals in the United States during World War II, Blount encountered many soldiers who had lost their arms in battle. She sought creative ways

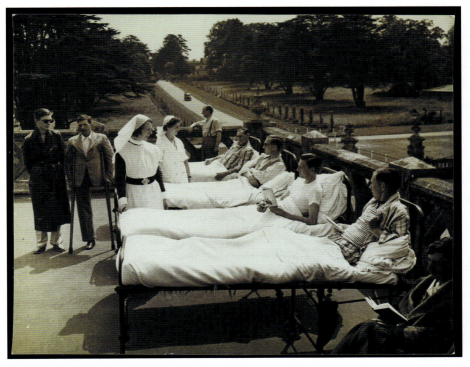

Soldiers from World War II (pictured here) used the self-feeding apparatus Bessie Blount created.

to help these soldiers regain their independence, including working with them to use their feet for tasks normally accomplished with their hands. However, she found that eating was the most difficult task for her patients to carry out on their own.

Designing the Solution

In response to this challenge, Blount created a device to assist them. She attached a tube to a food container that was outfitted with an electric motor, which could push food through the tube. The other end of the tube, when placed in the patient's mouth, would deliver a small amount of the food each time the patient bit down on it. This apparatus was largely successful; it was safe and reliable, and it could be used while the patient was either lying down in bed or sitting up in a wheelchair. However, the large size of the machine made it impractical for widespread use. Blount was unsuccessful marketing her tube-delivered feeding device. It proved too cumbersome to be considered for large-scale production and distribution.

"A black woman can invent something for the benefit of humankind."
—Bessie Blount Griffin

Refining the Invention

She turned her attention instead to a smaller, simpler apparatus to assist disabled people in eating. This device featured a brace worn around the patient's neck that could support a bowl or another receptacle in front. In 1948, she filed a patent application for her "Portable Receptacle Support." The patent was granted in 1951, giving her sole rights to this feeding apparatus.

Applying the Solution

While living in Newark, New Jersey, and teaching physical therapy at New York's Bronx Hospital, Blount attempted to market her newly patented device. She approached numerous medical supply manufacturers, and even the US Veterans Administration, but with no success. Unable to place her portable receptacle support into production in the United States, in 1952 Blount decided to sign the patent rights over to the French government, which used the device in its military hospitals.

The Impact of the Solution on Society

In the mid-1950s, Blount made the acquaintance of Theodore Edison, the great inventor Thomas Edison's son, when she became the caretaker of his mother-in-law. Blount soon began to talk to Theodore Edison about her inventions and ideas, and the two became good friends. Blount remained interested in developing new devices for hospital use. One device was a disposable cardboard emesis (vomit) basin that she had fashioned from newspaper, flour, and water, which was then baked into a hard form. Like her previous inventions, this basin did not attract favorable attention in the United States (where the metal kidney-shaped basins were preferred). It did, however, become standard in Belgian hospitals, where it remains in widespread use.

Bessie Blount Griffin (she had married in 1951) later turned her attention to **forensic science**. In 1969, she began conducting forensic

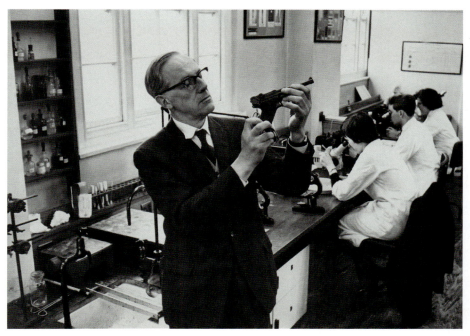

A man examines a gun in the Scotland Yard Forensic Science Laboratory in 1964.

research for the Vineland Police Department in New Jersey. She later worked in this capacity for the Norfolk and Portsmouth police departments in Virginia. By 1972, she had advanced to the position of chief document examiner in Portsmouth. Wanting to take her expertise to the next level, she applied in 1976 to the United States Federal Bureau of Investigation (FBI). Although she was turned down by the FBI, the following year she went on to work at Britain's Scotland Yard (the UK equivalent of the FBI), where she was the first black woman to receive training.

With the experience she had gained through years of forensic research, Blount eventually began her own forensic business specializing in examining historical records, especially African American slave documents and Native American treaties.

While her patented inventions did not necessarily receive worldwide acclaim, her reputation in the field of forensics expanded her legacy. She continued her role in Scotland Yard until her death in 2009, at the age of ninety-five. For her efforts in alleviating patient distress and restoring patient confidence post–World War II, she will always be remembered and admired, and her influence in medicine noted.

Timeline

1914
Bessie Blount born in Virginia

1941–1945
Blount invents a tube-delivered feeding device for injured veterans

1952
Blount signs patent rights for her portable receptacle support to the French government

1969
Blount begins conducting forensic research for various police departments

1977
Blount receives training at Britain's Scotland Yard

2009
Blount dies

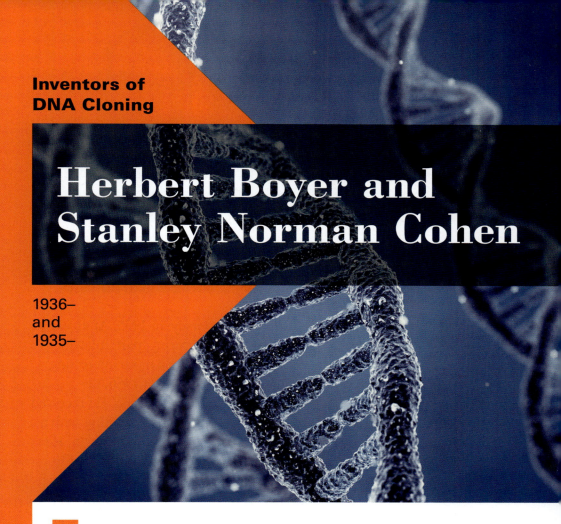

Inventors of DNA Cloning

Herbert Boyer and Stanley Norman Cohen

1936–
and
1935–

Technological advancements are made every day by people all over the world. Many inventions take years to create. Some start out as ideas from other sources and sound like something from a science fiction novel, but over time, they become integrated into society and influence humanity in ways not before imagined. Two inventors, Herbert Boyer and Stanley Cohen, shook the world by successfully cloning DNA from one organism to another. This revolutionized the way humans viewed reality and created controversy within the science community.

Two Inventors' Paths

Herbert Boyer and Stanley Norman Cohen were born one year apart. Both attended graduate school in Pennsylvania, and, as

25

Herbert Boyer (*left*) and Stanley Norman Cohen (*right*) shook the world with their invention of human DNA cloning.

adults, both moved to northern California, where they worked in biological research. Nonetheless, they did not meet until the 1970s, when they both went to Hawaii.

Cohen was born in Perth Amboy, New Jersey, in 1935. At an early age he became interested in science and engineering, particularly physics. Eventually he decided that medicine was a more interesting field, and after graduating from Rutgers University in 1956, he attended medical school at the University of Pennsylvania. He received his medical degree in 1960 and continued his medical training with a residency—the standard path to becoming a practicing physician. He decided, however, that he wanted to continue doing research, and in 1968 accepted a position at Stanford University in California.

Boyer was born in 1936 and grew up in Derry, a town in western Pennsylvania. He became interested in medicine while in high school and entered Saint Vincent College in nearby Latrobe to pursue its premed program. After a couple of years at Saint Vincent, Boyer decided that he would not make a good doctor and chose to become a researcher instead. He graduated in 1958 with a degree in biology and chemistry; he then began studies at the University of Pittsburgh, receiving his master's degree in 1960 and doctoral degree in 1963, both in bacteriology. Following three years of postgraduate work at Yale University, Boyer moved to the University of California at San Francisco, where he had been offered a job as an assistant professor.

The Ways of Bacteria

By the late 1960s, both Cohen and Boyer were studying a type of bacteria called *Escherichia coli*, usually abbreviated as *E. coli*.

This type lives in the digestive tract of most mammals, including humans. The bacterium is very easy to **cultivate**, making it a favorite for study among researchers.

Genetic information for most living creatures is contained in the lengthy deoxyribonucleic acid (DNA) molecule. Usually DNA is contained in a cell's nucleus, but some one-celled creatures, including *E. coli*, also have loops of DNA (plasmids) lying outside the nucleus. Certain strains of *E. coli* have unusual properties, such as resistance to antibiotic drugs. These properties are carried in the plasmid DNA, not in the **nuclear DNA**. Occasionally an *E. coli* bacterium will pass on these properties to another *E. coli* bacterium by giving a plasmid to the other bacterium.

Cohen was studying this process; in doing so, he and his team figured out a method to force an *E. coli* to absorb a plasmid that he had extracted from another *E. coli*. Using this method, he was able to make *E. coli* that were resistant to antibiotics. When the modified *E. coli* divided in order to reproduce, the next generation of *E. coli* also contained the plasmid introduced by Cohen and were also resistant to antibiotics.

Concurrently, Boyer was studying another property of *E. coli*—its defense mechanism against viruses. When *E. coli* is attacked by a virus, it counterattacks using a type of enzyme called a restriction enzyme. Restriction enzymes work by cleaving genetic molecules, causing genetic damage to the virus.

Boyer realized that different restriction enzymes target specific areas in the genetic code. In addition, once a restriction enzyme cut a section out of a genetic molecule, the cut ends of that section were "sticky" and their ends could join together to form a plasmid-like loop.

Defining the Problem

In 1972, both Cohen and Boyer traveled to Hawaii for a conference on plasmids. Boyer presented a paper on his discoveries about restriction enzymes; Cohen was immediately intrigued. The two men met for a late-night meal at a delicatessen, where they discussed the possibility of combining their research to devise a method of transplanting DNA from another species into *E. coli*.

Designing the Solution

At the time, many doubted that such a transplant was possible. Species are traditionally defined as a group of creatures that can produce viable offspring. Since members of different species cannot reproduce by conventional means, some sort of barrier was hypothesized on the genetic level. Nonetheless, Boyer and Cohen decided to try, and they agreed that their two research teams would work together. They used Boyer's knowledge of restriction enzymes to snip out a piece of genetic material and make a plasmid-like loop, and then used Cohen's expertise to transplant the newly created plasmid into *E. coli*. Within a few months, they were able to take a plasmid from another kind of bacteria carrying genes for antibiotic resistance and successfully implant it into *E. coli*.

Significantly, once the *E. coli* took up the foreign plasmid, it became resistant to antibiotics as well—just as had happened when *E. coli* took up plasmids from other *E. coli*. Thus, the origin of the plasmid DNA did not matter; the genetic instructions the DNA contained were followed by the *E. coli* just the same.

Boyer and Cohen published a paper on their work in 1973 that caused a sensation in academic circles. The significance of their discovery became clearer to the general public later that year when Boyer and Cohen manufactured a plasmid from the DNA of a toad and transplanted it into *E. coli*—demonstrating that what might appear to be vast differences between species, in fact, meant very little on a genetic level.

Their research suggested that humans could cobble together a living creature from the genetic material of vastly different species, an idea that many observers found both fascinating and troubling. The work of Boyer and Cohen sparked a still ongoing debate about how much humans should alter the existing natural order.

Applying the Solution

No one debated the business potential of Boyer and Cohen's discovery, however. Complex protein molecules are very difficult for chemists to manufacture in the laboratory, but the cells of living organisms manufacture complex proteins all the time. The

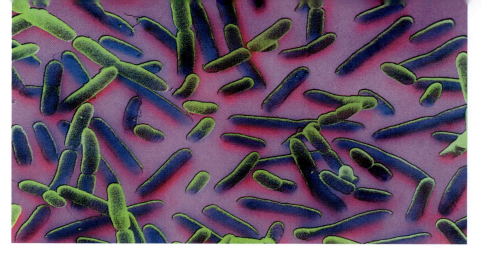

A magnified view of *E. coli*

instructions for manufacturing these proteins are contained in a cell's DNA. With Boyer and Cohen's method, genetic instructions to make a desirable protein could be snipped out and transplanted into *E. coli*. Then, the easy-to-grow bacteria could churn out large quantities of exceedingly pure protein for use in making valuable drugs.

The issue of profiting from academic research, typically a collaborative effort, is a delicate one. Academics are supposed to share information to encourage progress in the field. It is considered unseemly at best for an individual academic researcher to attempt to profit from any group effort, especially if the person tries to keep important techniques and methods secret in order to develop an idea commercially.

When the universities Boyer and Cohen worked for began to patent their techniques in the 1970s, both men repudiated any personal gain from the patents. Instead, the royalties for the patents went to Stanford and the University of California, which split some $27 million in royalty payments before the patents expired.

Maintaining Business

Although Cohen served as an adviser for some businesses, he mainly stayed in academia. He remained at Stanford, where he is a professor and head of the Stanley N. Cohen Laboratory, a genetics lab at Stanford's medical school.

Boyer continued teaching at UCSF. In 1976, however, he founded a for-profit biotechnology company, Genentech, Inc., which uses DNA cloning to make drugs (see sidebar). This action made him a divisive figure in the field of biotechnology.

Although the founding of Genentech most likely sped the development of life-saving drugs, the amount of money involved, and the resulting potential temptation to engage in dubious scientific and business practices, caused consternation in scientific circles.

For example, in September 1978, Genentech held a press conference announcing that it had manufactured human insulin.

Problems with Business

In 1975, Boyer was approached by venture capitalist Robert Swanson, who was convinced that DNA cloning could be used to develop valuable drugs. Swanson's enthusiasm convinced Boyer, and the two founded Genentech, Inc. the next year, with $1,000 of their own money.

In 1977, Genentech created the first *E. coli* that produced a human protein, the hormone somatostatin. Somatostatin had relatively limited commercial potential, but the following year, Genentech teamed up with pharmaceutical giant Eli Lilly and Company to develop a method to produce insulin, a hormone used to treat diabetes. At the time, diabetics who needed to inject insulin had to use insulin extracted from animals. Animal insulin was very expensive and could trigger deadly allergic reactions.

In 1978, Genentech genetically engineered *E. coli* to produce pure, safe, and relatively inexpensive human insulin, which Lilly began marketing in 1982. Genentech then used DNA cloning to manufacture the human growth hormone in 1979; this became the first drug the company marketed under its own name in 1985. The company went on to develop drugs used for bleeding disorders, clot-busting drugs used during heart attacks, and a variety of cancer medications.

The company's advances in the late 1970s helped fuel a biotechnology investing frenzy. In 1980, Genentech issued stock and became a public company; in the first twenty minutes of trading, the company's stock shot up from $35 a share to $89. As a result, Boyer's $500 founding investment became worth millions of dollars.

However, as many scientists pointed out, at that point the insulin had not been tested and the manufacturing process had not been perfected. From a business point of view, the announcement made sense: Genentech needed to attract money from investors in order to perfect its process; this announcement helped the company do that. In scientific circles, however, announcing a breakthrough before it has been perfected is often considered inappropriate because it could promote bad science.

Boyer and Cohen have received a number of prestigious awards for their discovery of DNA cloning, including the National Medal of Science (which Cohen received in 1988 and Boyer received two years later), the 1996 Lemelson-MIT Prize, the 2004 Albany Medical Center Prize in Medicine, and the Double Helix Medal in 2009. Despite having developed such an important and influential technology, neither has been awarded the Nobel Prize in Physiology or Medicine; many attribute this fact to a lingering unease in scientific circles with the way their discovery was developed.

The Impact of the Solution on Society

Outside the academic world, the development of DNA cloning has also caused unease, although for different reasons. One factor that has divided observers is the issue of patents. Boyer and Cohen's DNA cloning techniques were patented early on, and other researchers not only have patented various DNA cloning methods but have also patented the resulting genetically modified organisms themselves.

This practice was approved by the US Supreme Court in 1980. The court reasoned that it was necessary to protect the financial interests of the researchers, who spend considerable time and money developing genetically modified organisms. The idea that people can patent other forms of life, however, has troubled some, who view the practice as placing humans and their financial interests in an inappropriately dominant, almost godlike, position.

Other concerns have arisen as genetic engineering has been extended to include food crops. In particular, US farmers have embraced genetically modified crops. According to the US Department of Agriculture, in the United States around 93 percent of soybeans,

90 percent of cotton, and over 90 percent of feed corn grown in 2013 were genetically modified. Many of these crops have been modified to make the plants immune to certain herbicides or to make them produce their own insecticide, thereby lowering the cost to farmers of raising crops. Opponents of genetically modified crops argue that their safety to humans and to the environment has not been proved.

Despite controversies that have arisen due to genetic engineering, Boyer and Cohen's work remains important. Their invention has proved that people can modify and enhance nature's genetic makeup, for better or for worse, to behave in a way they want. Likewise, Boyer and Cohen have challenged previously existing thoughts and brought a new perspective regarding genes to the world of science.

Timeline

1935
Stanley Norman Cohen born in Perth Amboy, New Jersey

1936
Herbert Boyer born in Derry, Pennsylvania

1960
Cohen graduates from the University of Pennsylvania Medical School

1963
Boyer graduates with a doctoral degree in bacteriology from the University of Pittsburgh

1966
Boyer joins the University of California at San Francisco as an assistant professor

1968
Cohen accepts a position at Stanford University as a researcher

1972
Boyer and Cohen meet and decide to combine their research on *E. coli*

1973
Boyer and Cohen publish a paper on their research on DNA cloning

1976
Boyer founds Genentech, Inc., with Robert Swanson

1978
Genentech announces it has manufactured human insulin

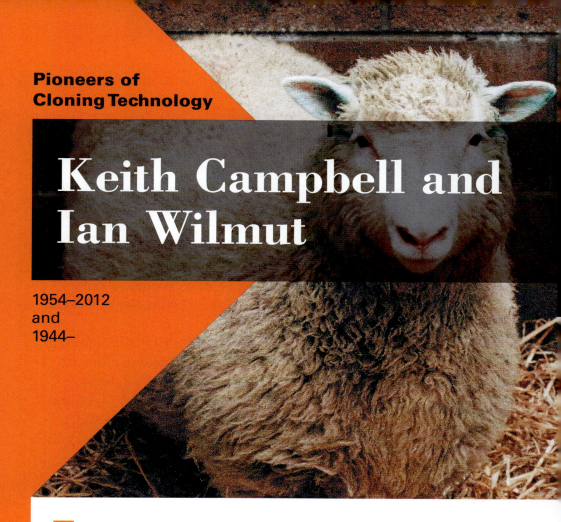

Pioneers of Cloning Technology

Keith Campbell and Ian Wilmut

1954–2012
and
1944–

For decades, the idea of cloning anything, let alone a medium-sized animal, was something that belonged in the realm of science fiction. People had been curious about what it would mean if such a feat was accomplished, and in the 1950s they had their answer, in the form of a tadpole. However, perhaps the best-known cloned animal appeared in 1997, when Dolly the sheep, the world's first animal cloned from adult cells, was born at the Roslin Institute in Scotland. She became an international sensation and the harbinger of an age where fiction truly met fact. Two scientists at the Roslin Institute, Keith Campbell and Ian Wilmut, took credit for making Dolly come to life. For their achievements, they became known around the world as pioneers in cloning technology. They and Dolly signaled the beginning of an age where cloning became more common, although controversial, and their achievements are recognized to this day.

Wilmut Grows Up

Ian Wilmut was born in 1944 and grew up in Coventry, England. Both his parents were schoolteachers. Wilmut enjoyed being outdoors and worked on farms during the weekends, eventually studying agriculture at the University of Nottingham. He abandoned his aspiration to be a farmer, however, because he felt that the business aspects of a successful career in agriculture were something he did not wish to take on. In the summer of 1966, Wilmut won an internship at an embryology laboratory, where he developed an avid interest in **embryos**.

After graduating from Nottingham in 1967, Wilmut continued to work in embryology, earning a doctorate from Cambridge University in 1971. As a graduate student, Wilmut focused on the **nascent** technology of freezing semen taken from livestock. In 1973, Wilmut was part of the scientific team that, for the first time, successfully implanted a frozen cow embryo into another cow and delivered a live, healthy calf named Frostie.

Roslin Calling

That same year, Wilmut accepted a job offer from a government-supported laboratory (now the Roslin Institute) in Roslin, Scotland. A prime center for agricultural research, Roslin hired Wilmut to study embryo development. In 1982, Roslin's leadership decided to change the institute's focus to the genetic engineering of sheep. At the time, genetic engineering was carried out by injecting DNA into zygotes (one-celled embryos). The zygotes, however, often did not take up the new DNA correctly, if at all. Consequently, Wilmut began looking for more efficient methods of creating genetically engineered animals.

Wilmut discovered that researchers working with certain breeds of mice had been able to isolate particular cells—embryonic stem (ES) cells—that could be grown in a culture, making them much easier to manipulate genetically. Once manipulated, the ES cells

Keith Campbell (*left*) and Ian Wilmut (*right*) speak at the Shaw Prize award presentation ceremony in Hong Kong in 2009.

could be injected into a mouse embryo, which would grow up to have genetically engineered eggs or sperm. Such mice could be bred with one another, creating genetically engineered offspring.

Defining the Problem

In early 1987, Wilmut attended an embryology conference in Dublin, Ireland. He heard about Danish scientist Steen Malte Willadsen, who had cloned a sheep in a process called nuclear transfer, which had been used by scientists since the 1950s.

In traditional fertilization, the nucleus of a sperm cell and the nucleus of an egg cell combine to create an embryo. In nuclear transfer, however, the nucleus of one cell is destroyed completely and replaced by the nucleus from another cell. Once that transfer takes place, the newly created cell is coaxed into dividing to make an embryo. Other scientists had used the technique to make clones, although the process seemed to work only when they used DNA from embryos in the earliest stages of development.

What Wilmut heard in Dublin, however, was that Willadsen had used DNA from embryos at a slightly later stage of development—around the same stage as embryonic stem cells. Wilmut realized that scientists at Roslin might be able to create a genetically engineered sheep by taking the DNA of a modified embryonic stem cell and implanting it directly into a zygote.

By 1989, Roslin had produced its first cloned lambs. Cells go through several regular stages, dividing, resting, and making copies of their own DNA so that they can divide again. Researchers at Roslin noticed that the stage a cell was at had a big impact on whether the cloning succeeded. In 1991, Wilmut submitted an advertisement to the respected scientific journal *Nature* for an expert on cell cycles. Among the respondents was scientist Keith Campbell.

Campbell's Early Years

Keith Campbell was born in 1954 and grew up in Birmingham, England. His father produced and sold agricultural seed. Campbell won a scholarship to high school but never took the exams required in Great Britain to attend college.

After graduating from high school, Campbell worked as a medical technician. He studied at night to get a technical degree, which he

How Cells Work

The body is made up of billions of cells, most of which have highly specialized functions. When specialized cells reproduce, they typically create more cells of the same tissue or organ—heart cells, for example, make only more heart cells.

All the cells in the body, however, are the direct descendants of one cell—the zygote, a one-celled embryo that divides and develops into the body. Cells such as a zygote, which can become any kind of cell, are called totipotent cells. As the embryo grows, the cells of the body undergo **differentiation**, a process in which they become specialized.

For many years, scientists believed that differentiation was irreversible—once a cell differentiated, it could never again become totipotent. When Keith Campbell was studying cancer at the Marie Curie Memorial Foundation, however, he began to question that belief. He noticed that tumors caused by cancer often contained a wide variety of cells—a tumor in the liver, for example, might contain hair or fingernails. Since cancer is caused by the body's own cells, Campbell began to suspect that differentiated cells were, indeed, able to become totipotent again.

received in 1975. With that degree, he was able to gain admission to Queen Elizabeth College in London, where he earned a bachelor's degree in microbiology in 1978. After working for a couple of years, Campbell decided to pursue a doctorate. He began studying cancer at the Marie Curie Memorial Foundation in London in 1980, but his interest soon turned to the more fundamental workings of cells.

Campbell moved to the University of Sussex, where he began studying how egg cells mature in frogs, work that focused intently on the chemistry of the cell cycle. After he received his doctorate in 1987, Campbell became interested in cloning. In 1991, he saw Wilmut's ad in *Nature*. He applied for and received the job at Roslin.

Designing the Solution

Both Campbell and Wilmut were interested in the question of how far along an embryo could develop before its DNA could no longer be used to make a clone. Campbell suspected that there was no limit; Wilmut believed there was a limit and wanted to determine when it was reached.

Campbell and Wilmut set up an experiment using three sets of embryonic cells: one set that came right from the embryo, one set that had been grown in the lab for a short time and had just begun to differentiate, and one set that had been growing in the lab for a long time and had clearly differentiated. The idea was to take the DNA from each of the three sets of cells, transplant it into new cells, and see which of those cells would develop into sheep.

For the experiment, Campbell developed a method of nuclear transfer that differed from the method used by researchers at Roslin. Before the nuclear transfer took place, Campbell chemically put all the cells into a deep resting stage. In addition, instead of transplanting the DNA into a zygote or another embryo, Campbell inserted it into a sheep's egg.

In a result that surprised even Campbell, sheep eggs that received DNA from all three groups of embryonic cells developed. In mid-1995, two surrogate-mother sheep each gave birth to a lamb: the lambs were called Megan and Morag.

Megan and Morag had come from the same culture of embryonic cells, so they were genetic clones of each other. More important, the embryonic cells they came from were the oldest ones in the experiment—they had been cloned from cells that had already differentiated. Wilmut and Campbell published their results in *Nature* in May 1996, with Campbell listed as the lead author.

Applying the Solution

Wilmut and Campbell decided to try cloning an adult cell. A for-profit subsidiary institute of Roslin—PPL Therapeutics, Ltd.—offered the use of some frozen cells that had been taken from the mammary gland of an adult Finn-Dorset sheep.

Using Campbell's techniques, Roslin's staff extracted DNA from the Finn-Dorset cells and transplanted it into egg cells taken from Scottish Blackface sheep; they made 277 embryos. Only twenty-nine of those embryos survived long enough to be implanted into surrogate mothers, which were also Scottish Blackface. Among those twenty-nine, only one pregnancy was carried to term. On July 5, 1996, a Scottish Blackface surrogate mother gave birth to a Finn-Dorset lamb. The scientists named the lamb Dolly—a reference to the country singer Dolly Parton.

Campbell and Wilmut wanted to publish news of Dolly's birth in *Nature* and attempted to keep the birth a secret, but news leaked out shortly before the article appeared in February 1997. Although Megan's and Morag's birth had received only limited publicity, Dolly's birth was headline news around the world.

In an agreement between Campbell and Wilmut, and also because Wilmut was head of the lab where Dolly had been made, Wilmut was credited as lead author of the paper on Dolly. Wilmut enjoyed talking to the media and operated as Roslin's chief spokesman about Dolly, enthusiastically participating in public debates over cloning.

The Impact of the Solution on Society

Much of the debate centered on the implications of Dolly's engineering for human cloning. In science fiction, human clones are

The Roslin Institute in Edinburgh, Scotland, where Dolly was born

typically perfect copies; in reality, making a perfect copy of a person is probably impossible. (Even identical twins are not exact copies of each other.) Wilmut and Campbell themselves opposed human cloning for a number of reasons, not least because the technology behind nuclear transfer was too unreliable to be applied to humans. In addition, both men claimed the likely psychological effects of human cloning make it undesirable, arguing that people (and perhaps clones themselves) would probably view clones simply as copies, rather than as fully individual, independent human beings.

In 1997, Campbell became head of embryology at PPL, helping to produce a number of other genetically engineered animals. Two years later he moved to the University of Nottingham, where he was a professor of animal development. In 2008, he won the Shaw Prize for Medicine and Life Sciences. He died in 2012 at the age of fifty-eight.

In the aftermath of Dolly's public appearance, Wilmut became something of a celebrity, writing popular articles and books about cloning. He became so closely associated in the public mind with the success of nuclear transfer that a minor scandal erupted in 2006 when he announced that Campbell deserved 66 percent of the credit for developing Dolly.

Wilmut remained at Roslin until 2005, when he was named head of the University of Edinburgh's Centre for Regenerative Medicine. That year, he received a license from British regulators to research human cloning—not, as Wilmut insisted, because he wished to clone people, but to help create cells that could be used to repair damage caused by accident or illness.

Following Wilmut and Campbell's success, many other scientists around the world have cloned different types of animals, including pigs, cats, dogs, and endangered species. However, cloning is still a mostly inefficient process, requiring much trial and error before success. Popular culture has also perpetuated the implications of human cloning. In sci-fi thriller *The Island* (2005), cloned humans are kept in a secret bunker until their donors need them for medical procedures. *Star Wars Episode II: Attack of the Clones* (2002) features armies of cloned Stormtroopers. There are questions concerning what human cloning would do to the world, as well as what possible health problems clones could suffer later in life. (Dolly herself was euthanized in 2003 after developing lung disease that was apparently unrelated to her cloning.) Nonetheless, cloning does have benefits: preserving rare, endangered, or extinct animals and enhancing genetic engineering. Only time will tell what the future holds for the continuation of cloning, but one thing is certain: Wilmut and Campbell's names will be forever remembered in its history.

Timeline

1944
Ian Wilmut born in Coventry, England

1954
Keith Campbell born; he grows up in Birmingham, England

1971
Wilmut earns a doctorate from Cambridge University

1987
Campbell earns a doctorate from the University of Sussex

1991
Campbell joins the staff at Roslin Institute

1995
The cloned lambs Megan and Morag are born

1996
The cloned lamb Dolly is born

2005
Wilmut receives a license to research human cloning

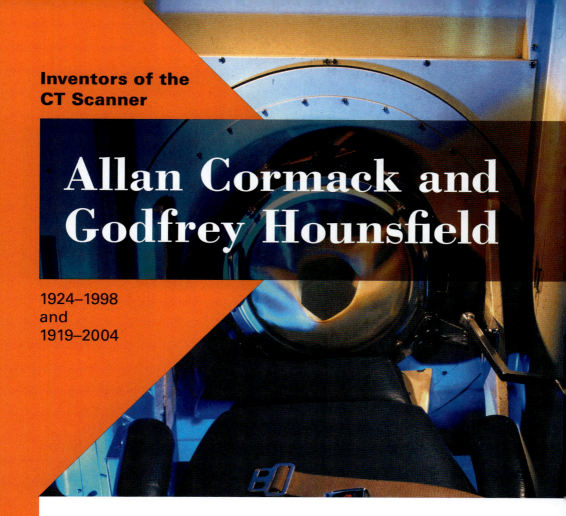

Inventors of the CT Scanner

Allan Cormack and Godfrey Hounsfield

1924–1998
and
1919–2004

Sometimes it takes more than one person and several years to invent something well and introduce it to the world. The computed tomography (CT) scanner is one such invention that came from the influence of several different inventors over several years. The two men attributed with inventing the CT scanner are Allan Cormack and Godfrey Hounsfield. Although they didn't meet until later in their careers, these men made significant contributions to the invention at different moments in history. Cormack was the first person to realize how the CT scanner would work, and Hounsfield was the first to build a working version. He and Cormack shared a Nobel Prize, awarded in 1979, and ever since, their names have been associated with the mechanism.

Godfrey Hounsfield's (*left*) and Allan Cormack's (*right*) independent research led to the invention of the CT scanner.

Starting in South Africa

Allan MacLeod Cormack was born in South Africa to Scottish parents in 1924. Cormack's father was an engineer with the post office, and the family moved often as his father was assigned to different locations. Cormack's father died in 1936, and the family then settled in Cape Town.

As a teenager, Cormack was fascinated by astronomy, but once he entered the University of Cape Town he decided it would be difficult to make a living as an astronomer, and he chose to study engineering instead. As his schooling progressed, Cormack discovered that he preferred physics, and he earned a bachelor's and then a master's degree in that discipline.

He moved to Cambridge University in England briefly for postgraduate study; there, he met his future wife, Barbara. Cormack felt he had to have a job that offered a salary high enough to support a family before he could marry, so he contacted the physics department at the University of Cape Town, which offered him a teaching position. Cormack, now married, returned to South Africa in 1950.

While working in Cape Town in 1955, Cormack received a call from the local Groote Schuur Hospital. At the time, South African law required that hospitals employ a physicist to supervise the use of radioactive isotopes in radiation therapy for patients suffering from diseases such as cancer. Groote Schuur's physicist had just resigned, and the hospital had called to see if Cormack would take the part-time job in addition to his teaching. He accepted.

Defining the Problem

During the six months he worked at Groote Schuur, Cormack noticed a rather significant shortcoming of radiation therapy. When attempting to determine how large a dose of radiation to give a patient, doctors relied on charts that were based on the assumption that every kind of tissue in the human body—bone, muscle, skin, fat—absorbed radiation equally. This was an assumption that Cormack and the doctors knew was false—materials of different density absorb radiation differently.

Cormack decided to create what would be essentially a map of the body that showed exactly how much radiation each kind of tissue absorbed. Patients would then receive no more radiation than they actually needed to treat their conditions.

Designing the Solution

While trying to figure out how to create this map, Cormack set up an experiment in 1957 in which he shot a beam of gamma rays through an aluminum-and-wood cylinder at a variety of angles into a detector. The experiment produced unusual data, and when Cormack investigated, he discovered that the aluminum cylinder, which he had thought was of a uniform thickness, in fact had a core peg of a density slightly different from the rest of the cylinder. Cormack had unwittingly detected this difference with his experiment.

Cormack quickly realized that a scanner that could detect such minute differences in density could have many important medical uses, particularly for diseases of the brain. One major drawback of traditional X-rays is that they cannot show the brain of a living patient because the dense bone of the skull blocks the radiation (see box, Working a CT Scanner). Before the advent of the CT scanner, if a person was thought to have a brain tumor, physicians would have to perform dangerous exploratory surgery before they knew exactly what was wrong.

Cormack set up another experiment, this time crafting a cylinder with an aluminum outer ring, a Lucite interior, and two aluminum pegs. Aluminum is denser than Lucite, and the cylinder was intended to represent the skull, the brain, and two tumors, respectively. By

Working a CT Scanner

A CT scanner and an X-ray machine obtain information by shooting radiation through a patient's body; however, a CT scanner is able to create far more detailed pictures of a patient's organs.

A conventional X-ray machine takes a picture as a camera would: an X-ray emitter is placed on one side of the body part concerned, a piece of film is placed on the other side, and a photograph-like image is created. That process, however, limits the quality of the image in two significant ways. First, X-ray film is not an especially sensitive detector of X-rays. Second, the resulting image is a composite of several images created as the X-rays pass through layers of organ and bone. Therefore, denser objects, such as the bones of the skull, conceal objects that are less dense, such as the brain.

In contrast, a CT scanner does not take a single reading of the area of the body being investigated; as the emitter is revolved around the body, extremely sensitive detectors take readings from many different angles. The result is an enormous quantity of data; a CT scanner typically produces tens of thousands of readings. To then create an image, the scanner requires a powerful computer to run the many sophisticated algorithms needed to translate all those readings into a single image.

Once the image is complete, it is remarkably detailed. It is almost impossible to tell one organ from another on an X-ray; but on a CT scan, different organs are easy to discern. Whereas a conventional X-ray of a head will simply show a skull, a CT scan will show the skull and the brain in tremendous detail. In addition, the digital image produced by a CT scan can be manipulated on a computer so that a three-dimensional image can be virtually rotated or sliced as needed.

shooting radiation at the "skull" from many different angles, he easily found the "tumors" within. Cormack, who had by now taken a position as a physics professor at Tufts University in Medford, Massachusetts, published two articles in the journal *Applied Physics* on his groundbreaking discovery, one in 1963 and one in 1964.

"There was virtually no response," he later recalled. The implications of the physicist's experiment seemed to be unappreciated by manufacturers of medical devices. Part of the problem was that the technology was clearly going to require expensive, powerful computers to work, and no manufacturer was willing to invest in an untried technology. In addition, Cormack was busy with his job; named chairman of the physics department at Tufts in 1968, he did not have the time to vigorously promote what was essentially a side project.

Cormack's breakthrough seemed fated to remain obscure. He was not alone: at least two other scientists have also been credited with discovering many of the underlying principles of the CT scanner, but they, too, were unable to interest any company in manufacturing the new technology. Only when Hounsfield made a similar breakthrough did this situation change.

Raised in the Country

Born in 1919, Godfrey Newbold Hounsfield grew up on a farm near Nottinghamshire, England. The youngest of five children, Hounsfield showed an early interest in machinery and science: as a teenager he built a record player out of spare parts, and from time to time he jumped off the tops of haystacks wearing a homemade glider. He was less interested in his schoolwork, however, and he did not do well enough to be admitted to a university.

When World War II broke out, Hounsfield's interest in airplanes led him to volunteer for the Royal Air Force (RAF). He started taking RAF courses in radio and radar mechanics, and he showed such aptitude that he was made a lecturer on radar. Following the war, Hounsfield received a grant that allowed him to attend Faraday House Electrical Engineering College in London, from which he graduated in 1951.

Right Place, Right Time

That same year, Hounsfield went to work for EMI, a London music company that had branched out into electronics. Beginning around 1958, Hounsfield led a team at EMI that built Britain's first all-transistor computer. A few years later, Hounsfield was given the opportunity to pick a field of research, and he chose pattern recognition.

In 1967, while thinking about various problems in pattern recognition, Hounsfield made a mental leap similar to the one Cormack had made. Hounsfield realized that penetrating an object with radiation at different angles would produce data that could be used to construct an image of the object's interior.

Applying the Solution

Unlike Cormack, Hounsfield did not spend the next several years vainly trying to interest people in his project. As a respected researcher at a technologically oriented company that was willing to fund his ideas, Hounsfield had the means to build and perfect the first CT scanner.

Hounsfield began much like Cormack, shooting gamma rays at inanimate objects. Soon he switched to passing X-rays through the brains of humans and cows. The clarity of the resulting images was startling: the scans showed the interior structure of the brain in remarkable detail. Hounsfield then conducted his first scan on a human patient, a woman who was suspected of having a brain tumor. Although the scan took fifteen hours, the results were impressive—the tumor showed up as a large, dark spot that was easy even for someone with no medical training to see. The woman had surgery to remove the tumor.

The Impact of the Solution on Society

In 1972, EMI unveiled the first commercially available CT scanner to the world. Despite its high price, initially more than $300,000, the device caused a sensation. Soon, other medical-device firms were offering their own scanners and looking to previously neglected scientists like Cormack for help in improving the devices.

Cormack and Hounsfield met in Sweden seven years later, when they received the 1979 Nobel Prize in Physiology or Medicine.

Godfrey Hounsfield (*center*) receives the Nobel Prize for Medicine in 1979.

Although both men spoke out in favor of advancing medical imaging, neither one radically altered his career to pursue the field. Cormack remained a professor at Tufts and died in 1998; Hounsfield remained at EMI, was knighted in 1981, and died in 2004.

In the late 1980s, two new scanners were invented that expanded the functionality of the CT scanner: a superfast scanner that can take pictures of a heart between beats and a spiral CT scanner that can capture images of large portions of the body in a very short time.

Thousands of CT scanners are now in use in the United States, and they are increasingly applied for nonmedical purposes. Archaeologists use CT scanners to examine the interior of historical artifacts; security personnel at airports and elsewhere use them to scan suspect packages and bags. Indeed, CT scans have become so popular in recent years that medical organizations have felt the need to suggest limits on their use because of worries that patients will be overexposed to X-rays.

There is no doubt CT scanners have benefited the medical field and saved many lives. Without individuals like Cormack and

Hounsfield, and their CT scanners, the medical industry would perhaps be suffering for new technology. However, with these devices available, lives can continue to be saved and the medical field can continue to expand.

Timeline

1919
Godfrey Newbold Hounsfield born near Nottinghamshire, England

1924
Allan MacLeod Cormack born in South Africa

1939–1945
Hounsfield lectures on radar in Royal Air Force during World War II

1950
Cormack accepts teaching position at University of Cape Town

1951
Hounsfield graduates from engineering college and begins work at EMI

1957
Cormack begins imaging experiments

1958
Hounsfield's team at EMI builds Great Britain's first all-transistor computer

1963–1964
Cormack publishes papers on his experiments

1967
Hounsfield gets idea for CT scanner and begins experiments

1968
Cormack named chairman of Tufts University's physics department

1972
EMI unveils the first commercially available CT scanner

1979
Cormack and Hounsfield awarded the Nobel Prize

1998
Cormack dies

2004
Hounsfield dies

Inventor of the Magnetic Resonance Imaging Scanner

Raymond Damadian

1936–

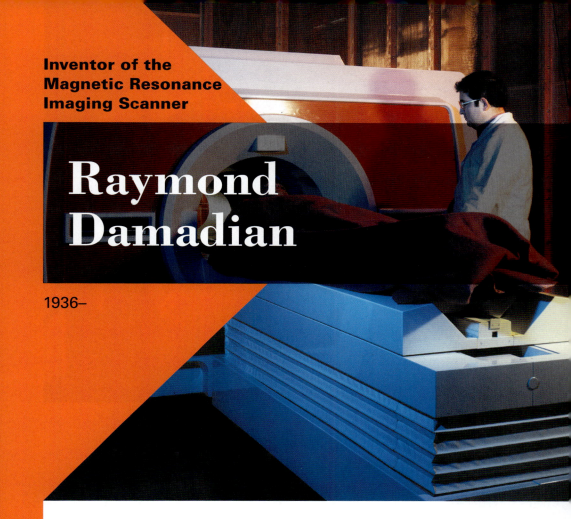

Throughout the centuries, many inventions have changed the way people live and work. The medical industry, too, has seen revolutionary inventions that have challenged thinking and made it possible to diagnose complex medical conditions. One of the most influential and important inventions in the nineteenth century was the magnetic resonance imaging (MRI) scanner. Its inventor, Raymond Damadian, helped improve medical practice all around the world. The MRI allowed people to see more clearly into the human body, thus enabling doctors to diagnose problems earlier and save the lives of their patients.

Raymond Damadian poses with the MRI machine prototype Indomitable in 1977.

A Young Inventor

Raymond Vahan Damadian was born on March 16, 1936, in Forest Hills, New York. As a child growing up in New York City, he entered the Juilliard School of Music Pre-College Program, where he studied violin for eight years. Damadian began his university training at the University of Wisconsin on a Ford Foundation scholarship when he was fifteen. While completing a degree in mathematics, he determined that medicine would offer more interesting career options. After graduating in 1956, Damadian entered the Albert Einstein College of Medicine in New York, receiving his medical degree in 1960.

Defining the Problem

While completing his medical degree at Einstein, Damadian made a crucial decision. He had entered medical school intending to specialize in internal medicine with a view toward becoming a clinical practitioner. He changed his mind, however, deciding to concentrate on medical research rather than on practicing medicine. One of his motivations came from watching his grandmother die of breast cancer. Damadian determined to make a difference in the way that cancer might be detected and thereby, perhaps, cured.

Upon receiving his MD, Damadian served as a fellow in **nephrology** at Washington University School of Medicine in St. Louis and then as a fellow in biophysics at Harvard University's School of Medicine. At Harvard, he conducted advanced research in physics, physical chemistry, and mathematics. He went on to receive further training in the field of physiological chemistry at the School of Aerospace Medicine in San Antonio, Texas, while serving as a captain in the US Air Force. Upon returning from active duty in 1967, Damadian accepted a faculty position in internal medicine and biophysics at the State University of New York (SUNY) Medical School Downstate.

Designing the Solution

As a professor at SUNY, Damadian began working with a technology called nuclear magnetic resonance (NMR) spectroscopy. The NMR process involved placing an atom in a stable magnetic field, where its nucleus would absorb electromagnetic waves of radio frequency. Different types of nuclei would absorb these waves differently. Each nucleus would then reemit radio waves at a unique, predictable frequency, allowing researchers to analyze the composition of various substances with greater accuracy.

Isidor Isaac Rabi, a physicist at Columbia University, first discovered the NMR method in 1938, for which he was awarded a Nobel Prize in 1944. Soon thereafter, physicists Felix Bloch of Stanford University and Edward Purcell at Harvard extended the method to analyze protons, part of the nucleus of an atom. Within a decade of Rabi's first discovery, NMR had become a standard tool for physicists and chemists to analyze substances. Although NMR spectroscopy had been used for identifying a wide range of substances, it had not been considered for use on humans.

Damadian first experimented with this technology while conducting research into sodium and potassium in living cells. He quickly saw the promise that NMR technology held out for diagnostic medicine. Specifically, he began to investigate how NMR could reveal the changes and differences between healthy cells and cancerous cells. In 1971, while experimenting with mice, Damadian discovered that NMR signals produced by cancerous cells lasted much longer than signals emitted by healthy cells. He published his findings in the journal *Science* and suggested that magnetic resonance scanning could be used to diagnose cancer early enough to slow or halt the disease's spread. He soon applied for a patent for a device that would allow doctors to use magnetic fields and radio waves to examine the human body for cancerous tumors. Damadian was awarded this patent in 1974.

An MRI in Action

How did nuclear magnetic resonance become a way for creating images that doctors could examine? The answer lies in water.

The human body is about two-thirds water. Each water molecule is made up of hydrogen and oxygen atoms. When exposed to a magnetic field, the nuclei of hydrogen atoms react by changing their position slightly. As the magnetic waves pulse, the hydrogen atoms indicate specific differences in their nuclei as they react to the magnetic field and then return to their "normal" state. These differences (or oscillations) are detected through the resonance waves the nuclei emit.

When we become sick, the water content of our organs and tissues changes. Raymond Damadian sought a way to show these changes in a three-dimensional image that would demonstrate the chemical structure of organs or tissues. Although he could analyze these data accurately, his method for processing the data into three-dimensional images of the chemical structure of tissue and organs was less successful. Other researchers, especially Paul Lauterbur, drew on Damadian's discoveries to create superior imaging technology.

Applying the Solution

Not everyone shared Damadian's enthusiasm for a magnetic resonance scanner for humans. After failing to get funding through the National Institutes of Health and other government agencies, he finally managed to secure some funds from private backers to keep his NMR work going. After years of work, Damadian and his students unveiled their first machine, called Indomitable, which was capable of doing a magnetic resonance scan of the chest. Indomitable received wider attention in July 1977, after one of Damadian's students sat inside it for several hours while rudimentary images showed the student's heart and chest cavity.

In 1978, Damadian formed a company, FONAR (from Field fOcused Nuclear mAgnetic Resonance), to build MRI scanners. The first commercial scanner was released in 1980. The Food and Drug Administration approved Damadian's machine in 1984. Since that time, advances by Damadian and others have led to increasingly refined scanning technology that allows doctors to examine the human body in great detail.

Inventors Dispute

Damadian's first devices, built on the model of Indomitable, failed to sell because they produced low-quality images. While Damadian was developing his MRI scanner in the early 1970s, another medical researcher, Paul Lauterbur, at the State University of New York at Stony Brook, began to look at the results of Damadian's work and concluded that his method of generating images was flawed. Lauterbur proposed an alternative method using a second, weaker magnetic field that could be controlled to vary its position in relation to the first magnetic field, creating a two-dimensional image. Lauterbur's results were superior to Damadian's, and eventually Damadian himself adopted Lauterbur's methods for his production of MRI scanners at FONAR.

The two men never collaborated in their research and were, in fact, often at odds with each other. Damadian felt that Lauterbur had unfairly ignored his contributions, as Lauterbur attempted to claim the development of MRI scanning technology for himself. In a paper he published in the journal *Nature* in March 1973, Lauterbur demonstrated images achieved by his magnetic resonance scanning without any reference to Damadian or his work. This began a tense relationship between the two men that culminated in a controversial awarding of the 2004 Nobel Prize in Physiology or Medicine to Lauterbur and fellow British researcher Peter Mansfield for development of the MRI. Although the Nobel committee could have awarded the prize to three researchers, Damadian was omitted. He subsequently took out several full-page ads in newspapers protesting his exclusion and urging readers to express outrage to the Nobel committee.

Paul Lauterbur challenged Damadian's claim of inventing the MRI machine.

The Impact of the Solution on Society

Some maintain that Damadian is the true inventor of MRI because he was the first to adapt known NMR principles to medicine. Supporters of Damadian also point out that he was the first to recognize that cancerous cells emit signals of longer duration than healthy cells when scanned. Others, recognizing the flaws in Damadian's images (the crucial "I" of MRI), consider that the most important developments in MRI research rightfully belong to Lauterbur and Mansfield. Another factor often cited as a reason for Damadian's exclusion from the Nobel Prize is his religious philosophy. As a **creationist**, Damadian is part of a minority in the scientific world. Some creationists have decried the Nobel snub as prejudice against their beliefs.

Damadian has been recognized elsewhere for his contributions to MRI technology. He was awarded, jointly with Lauterbur, the National Medal of Technology by President Ronald Reagan in 1988, "for their independent contributions in conceiving and developing the application of magnetic resonance technology to medical uses including whole-body scanning and diagnostic imaging." Damadian was inducted into the National Inventors Hall of Fame in 1989, and in 2001 he received the Lemelson-MIT Lifetime Achievement Award. The first scanning machine Damadian built is part of the Smithsonian Institute's permanent collection.

MRIs are used frequently today. They can detect muscle injuries, abnormalities in tissue and cells, and brain activity. Many athletic facilities even have their own MRI scanners. Raymond Damadian's influence on the medical industry and the way some illnesses are diagnosed is felt throughout the world. His invention will be remembered as a medical landmark, and he will always be remembered as a major player in the field of medicine.

Timeline

1936
Raymond Vahan Damadian born in Forest Hills, New York

1960
Damadian graduates from Albert Einstein College of Medicine

1967
Damadian joins the faculty at SUNY Medical School

1971
Damadian publishes his research about NMR signals

1977
The first NMR images are taken

1978
Damadian forms FONAR company to build MRI scanners

1980
The first commercial scanner is released

2003
Approximately seventy-five million MRI scans are performed in one year

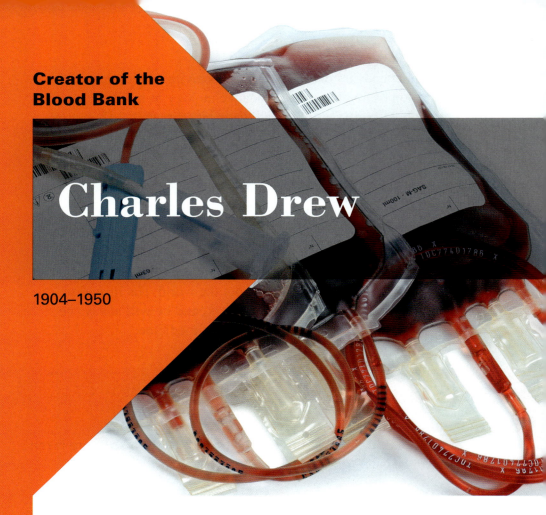

Creator of the Blood Bank

Charles Drew

1904–1950

Many inventors and inventions have come and gone in the course of history. Some inventions have left an indelible mark, while others have faded into obscurity. Others, such as key medical inventions, have been the difference between life and death. Charles Drew, an African-American doctor, made one of the most profound inventions of the twentieth century, with the creation of the first blood banks. These stores of blood became integral to saving human lives and continue to do so today.

Beginnings

Charles Drew was born in Washington, DC, on June 3, 1904, the oldest of the five children of Richard and Nora Drew. Both

Charles Drew in a laboratory in Washington, DC, in 1946

athletically gifted and very enterprising, Drew was frequently voted best athlete and earned four varsity letters at Dunbar High School. When he was not on the football field or the track, he was running a business with his friends, selling newspapers.

Drew's athletic gifts earned him a scholarship to Amherst College in 1922, but coming from a poor family, he still had to wait tables to pay his way. For his first two years at Amherst, he excelled on the sports field: he was a champion quarterback and baseball player and was an outstanding hurdler. However, this early success came at the expense of his grades. Gradually, he focused more on his studies, managing to earn 100 percent on his final chemistry exam. When he graduated from Amherst in 1926, Drew was still not sure what he would do with his life. For the next two years, he worked as a science teacher and athletics coach at Morgan State College in Baltimore, Maryland. He and the school were successful— the college's basketball and football teams won championships.

When Drew decided to apply to medical school, the money he had saved at Morgan State proved useful. He attended McGill University in Montreal, Canada, where he studied with eminent British anatomy professor Dr. John Beattie. Drew's brilliance was soon recognized: when he graduated in 1933 with degrees in medicine and surgery, he ranked second of 127 students. Now a doctor, he worked as an intern in Montreal before moving back to the United States—to Howard University in Washington, DC, in 1935.

A Safe Place for Blood

While working as an instructor in pathology at Howard, Drew won a Rockefeller Foundation Fellowship to study at Columbia University in New York City. There, between 1938 and 1940, he began his important research into blood—and he soon became a world expert on **transfusions**. In 1939, he met his future wife, Lenore. Together they would have three children. In 1940, he published everything he had discovered while at Columbia in his doctoral dissertation, "Banked Blood: A Study in Blood Preservation."

Working for Equality

When Charles Drew died in 1950, the United States had two separate medical systems: one for blacks and one for whites. In Birmingham, Alabama, a center of many civil rights struggles, black physicians were excluded from jobs in the city hospitals until 1954. Black residents were given access to those same hospitals only a decade later, with the passage of the 1964 Civil Rights Act.

That law came into force partly through the campaigns of black doctors, who were seeking to overturn racial segregation in the medical system. One of them was Paul D. Cornely at the University of Michigan. During the 1940s and 1950s, Cornely ran a project to study the different treatment of blacks and whites in American hospitals. He carefully documented what he found and publicized the shocking inequalities in scores of articles and many public meetings. Such campaigning increased the pressure for change. In the 1950s, another Michigan graduate, Hubert Eaton, applied for a physician's post at the local hospital for whites. When he was turned down, as he expected, he filed suit and began a long series of legal challenges until he won a victory in 1964 in the federal appeals court.

Thanks to these and other determined doctors, and the earlier efforts of pioneers such as Charles Drew, that year marked the beginning of the end for racial segregation in hospitals. When the Civil Rights Act was passed in 1964, federal government funds could no longer be given to organizations or activities that segregated blacks and whites. Thus, when the Medicare program was introduced in 1966, hospitals had to end segregation or lose their federal funding. In a matter of months, one thousand hospitals quickly and efficiently ended segregation—and set out on the road to racial equality.

Although blood transfusions were routine at the time, they were problematic. People have different types (or groups) of blood, and in most cases blood donated by a person of one group cannot be given to a person of a different group. In Drew's time, blood had a maximum storage life of one week and could be stored for only two days in a refrigerator before it began to break down. Thus, any stockpiling of blood for future emergencies was impossible.

Defining the Problem

During the course of his research, Drew realized that blood transfusions could be carried out in an entirely different way. Blood has two main components: the red blood cells that carry oxygen and other vital supplies to different parts of the body, and plasma, the pale, watery part of the blood, wherein the red blood cells are suspended. The red blood cells make one blood group different from another and one person's blood incompatible with another's; the red blood cells also break down fastest. However, everyone has the same type of blood plasma.

Charles Drew saw that it was relatively easy to divide blood into its different components and store them separately. When the plasma was separated from the red blood cells, he found it could be stored under refrigeration much longer. He began to theorize that blood plasma could be used by itself for emergency transfusions or stored separately and recombined with red blood cells at some later date. Drew proved that his idea could work by setting up a blood bank at Columbia University.

Designing the Solution

As the 1930s came to a close, Charles Drew married Lenore Robbins on September 29, 1939. That same month, the nations of Europe were plunged into World War II.

Several months later, Drew became the first African-American student to earn a doctorate in medical science from Columbia University with his work on blood banking. His expertise in blood transfusion now came into its own. His former anatomy professor,

John Beattie, had returned to England, where he was working on the difficult problem of organizing blood transfusions for soldiers injured in the war. As fighting intensified, the need for blood was great. Beattie sent Drew a telegram in New York City, asking him to help the British by supplying five thousand packets of blood plasma.

Within weeks, Charles Drew was organizing a large-scale lifesaving operation that became known as Blood for Britain: blood was donated in New York City hospitals, and the plasma was separated, banked, and then shipped to Britain, where it helped to save the lives of many thousands injured in the conflict. The project was an immediate and spectacular success.

Applying the Solution

As it became more apparent that the United States might enter the war, a similar operation was needed at home. Thus, in February 1941, Charles Drew was appointed director of the first American Red Cross blood bank at Presbyterian Hospital in New York City. There, he was in charge of collecting, storing, and distributing blood for the US Army and Navy. Drew remained in this post only nine months. A military directive required him to store blood collected from black donors separately from the blood donated by whites. Drew was appalled: skin color had no connection to blood. The order meant that injured soldiers, sailors, and airmen would have to wait for blood transfusions from those of the same racial type and that many people—black and white—could therefore die unnecessarily. Drew resigned in protest.

After leaving the Red Cross, Drew found a new way to save lives—by helping to train physicians and surgeons at Howard University. From 1941 until 1950, he was professor of medicine, and his department quickly gained a reputation for first-class training and academic excellence. He also worked as a surgeon at Freedman's, the teaching hospital linked to Howard, where he became the medical director in 1946.

During the 1940s, Drew published more than a dozen important papers on blood and transfusions, which helped to secure his reputation as an international authority. During the next few years, his expertise was recognized with a variety of honors and awards. In 1944, his work on blood plasma earned him the Spingarn Medal from the National Association for the Advancement of Colored People. The following year, he was granted honorary degrees by Virginia State College and Amherst College. He was elected a Fellow of the International College of Surgeons in 1946.

The Impact of the Solution on Society

On April 1, 1950, Charles Drew was driving three of his colleagues to a medical conference in Alabama. As they passed Burlington, North Carolina, he fell asleep at the wheel. The car swerved and rolled over, and Drew was thrown out of the vehicle. The car tipped on top of him, causing massive injuries to Drew's head and chest. The other doctors in the car had only minor injuries. Drew was immediately rushed to the hospital in Burlington, but the doctors there were unable to save him and he died shortly afterward.

Rumors soon began to circulate that Drew had been admitted to the hospital for a blood transfusion but was turned away because he was a black man. This would have been a supreme irony, given Drew's background and his personal battle for racial equality. It would not have been unusual, however, given the inequalities in medical care for African Americans at the time. Later, the rumor was proved to be unfounded: one of the other men traveling in the car, John Ford, confirmed that Drew was simply too badly injured to survive. According to Ford, Drew had in fact received "the very best of care" and "all the blood in the world could not have saved him."

A Red Cross poster advertising blood donation during World War II

Charles Drew was more than just the inventor of the blood bank. He was an athlete, an accomplished medical professional, and a teacher. He spent his life working to help others and to make the world a better place for everyone to live in. His contribution to the medical industry did revolutionize the way blood transfusions were performed, and today his procedures are used in hospitals around the world. Drew's legacy lives on in his accomplishments and the mark he left on society.

Timeline

1904
Charles Drew born in Washington, DC

1933
Drew graduates from McGill University

1935
Drew joins the faculty at Howard University

1938
Drew begins blood research at Columbia University

1941
Drew is made director of American Red Cross blood bank but leaves in protest soon after

1946
Drew becomes medical director of teaching hospital at Howard University

1950
Drew dies

Inventors of Human In Vitro Fertilization

Robert Edwards and Patrick Steptoe

1925–2013
and
1913–1988

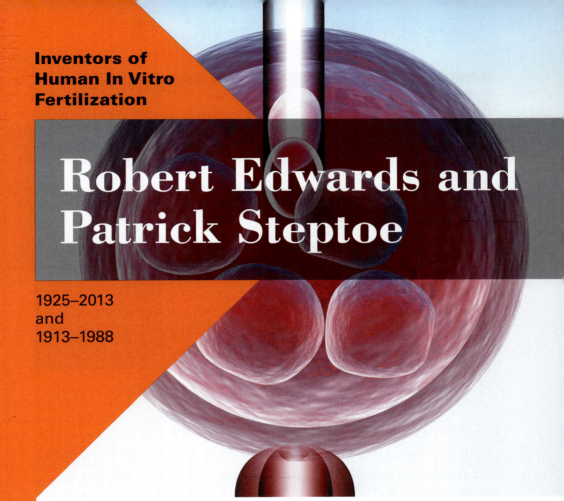

In the twentieth century, medical practice changed around the world with many new inventions and discoveries. There were new techniques and procedures being speculated and researched, and eventually some of those were put into practice. One such technique was a new way of conceiving a child through a process called in vitro fertilization (IVF). Two scientists, Robert Edwards and Patrick Steptoe, made headlines in 1978 when Steptoe delivered a girl named Louise Brown, who had been conceived through this method. Although originally controversial at the time, IVF led to other reproductive technologies and gave hope to people who could not bear children.

Patrick Steptoe (*left*) and Robert Edwards (*right*) in 1979

Edwards Growing Up

Robert Edwards was born in Leeds, England, in 1925, but grew up in the industrial city of Manchester. His family had very little money; however, Edwards was a bright student, and when he was eleven, he was offered a scholarship to a prestigious school that his mother insisted he accept.

Following the outbreak of World War II in 1939, Edwards, along with many other British children and teenagers, was evacuated to the countryside because of German bomb attacks on British cities. Edwards would later credit the experience with piquing his interest in the natural world. When he was old enough, Edwards joined the army, serving until 1949.

After his discharge, Edwards attended college at the University of Wales at Bangor. Initially majoring in agriculture, he switched to zoology in his senior year. Upon hearing of a friend's plans to do postgraduate study in genetics at Edinburgh University, Edwards decided to follow suit. He applied and was accepted, earning a doctorate in 1955.

Patrick Steptoe's Beginnings

Patrick Steptoe was born in 1913 in Whitney, England. His father was a church organist, and Steptoe himself was an adept piano player. His mother was a supporter of women's rights, and she instilled in Steptoe a profound interest in the welfare of women.

After graduating from secondary school, Steptoe attended St. George's Medical School in London, finishing in 1939, just at the beginning of World War II. He volunteered for the navy. During the war, his ship was torpedoed off the island of Crete. Steptoe swam for two hours until he was captured by the Italian navy; he spent two years as a prisoner of war. After the war, Steptoe returned to London, where he worked as a gynecologist. Deciding that it was too difficult to become professionally established there, in 1951 he moved to Oldham, a fairly remote town in northern England.

Defining the Problem

Oldham had few medical professionals, and for years Steptoe struggled to provide even basic care to women in the area. Steptoe began seeing more and more cases of infertility. At the time, exploratory surgery was commonly done to determine why a woman was infertile. Steptoe sought a less extreme alternative to solving issues related to infertility. In 1959, he heard of the new laparoscopic technique, which had been developed in France. He obtained a laparoscope (a thin fiber-optic tube) and eventually became one of Great Britain's foremost experts on the device, publishing a textbook on the subject in 1967.

First Attempts at IVF

Edwards, on the other hand, remained in London and was doing his own investigating into infertility. By 1960, he had started a family and was working as a researcher. His friends included an infertile couple who liked to come over and visit Edwards's daughters.

Prompted by the couple's plight, Edwards began to consider the possibility of using animal reproduction techniques to help infertile people. At the time, researchers were able to take eggs from a female animal, fertilize them in a lab, and then transplant the resulting embryo into the animal's womb. When successful, the procedure, known as in vitro fertilization, would result in pregnancy and birth. Edwards thought that he might be able to perform the same procedure with humans.

Edwards, who had moved to Cambridge University in 1963, began working on fertilizing a human egg in the lab. At that time, the general belief was that human fertilization could happen only inside the body; in 1965, however, Edwards succeeded in fertilizing a human egg outside the body. When he tried to repeat the experiment, however, he failed. By 1967, Edwards had still not fertilized another egg in the lab. He decided that human sperm must somehow be altered during sexual intercourse to make fertilization possible. The only way to obtain and study such sperm would be to ask a female volunteer to submit to dangerous abdominal surgery.

In the fall of 1967, however, Edwards happened upon a journal article describing a new surgical technique, laparoscopy, which uses a laparoscope inserted into the abdomen to provide light for special tube-shaped surgical instruments. Only small incisions were made during the procedure, making laparoscopy far less traumatic to patients than traditional surgery. The author of the article on laparoscopy was Patrick Steptoe.

Edwards and Steptoe Together

Edwards called Steptoe and explained how he would like to use laparoscopy to perform IVF in people. Unlike most of the gynecologists Edwards had spoken to, Steptoe was happy to help. Edwards, however, realized that working with Steptoe would be extremely challenging—Oldham and Cambridge were more than 160 miles (257 km) apart, and only small, winding country roads connected them. Edwards did not call Steptoe again.

The next year, Edwards attended a medical conference, where he ran into Steptoe. Steptoe was still excited by Edwards's idea, and Edwards realized that if he wanted human IVF to move forward, he needed someone with Steptoe's expertise. He made the first of what would prove to be countless round trips to Oldham later that year, eventually setting up a lab in the hospital where Steptoe worked.

Designing the Solution

In Cambridge, a student of Edwards's developed a culture fluid that promoted fertilization in hamster eggs. The fluid also worked with human eggs. Although this culture fluid settled the problem of fertilization, Steptoe continued to play a crucial role in the future of IVF: his infertility patients volunteered to provide Edwards with eggs, which Steptoe retrieved through laparoscopy. Edwards eventually

Facing Problems

For much of the 1970s, Edwards and Steptoe were stumped by implantation, which occurs easily in nature. When an egg is fertilized, the resulting embryo implants itself in the uterus, which has built up a thick, blood-rich lining to support it. When Edwards and Steptoe tried to implant embryos in patients, however, the implant would fail and a pregnancy would not occur.

The cause of the pregnancy failures was eventually attributed to the fertility drugs Edwards and Steptoe would give the patients. Such drugs would cause several eggs to mature at once, making retrieval with a laparoscope easier. The drugs, however, would also accelerate the mother's menstrual cycle; by the time the embryo was returned to the womb, the uterus was about to shed the lining that the embryo needed to sustain itself.

At first, Edwards and Steptoe simply modified the drug regime. In 1975, one of their patients conceived, but success proved fleeting. Steptoe determined that the embryo had implanted itself in a fallopian tube, not the uterus. Such a pregnancy would have been lethal for both the mother and the baby, and the pregnancy had to be terminated.

After two more years of failure, Edwards decided that they should not use fertility drugs at all, especially since Steptoe was skilled enough with the laparoscope to retrieve single eggs. Instead, patients were constantly monitored for the hormonal changes indicating natural ovulation, and Steptoe's team was placed on call around the clock to remove the eggs whenever they were produced.

devised a culture in which the fertilized eggs could develop into embryos. The next step was to actually implant the embryo into a woman's womb to create a pregnancy, but this procedure would require a better-equipped lab than the one in Oldham.

Applying the Solution

Edwards and Steptoe applied for funding from the British government to outfit a lab near Cambridge. Edwards had been publishing papers about his progress, however, and human IVF was proving to be an extremely controversial idea. It was decried by religious leaders as an attempt by men like Edwards to take on the role of God. In 1969, a survey of Americans found that more than two-thirds thought that such fertilization technology would mean "the end of babies born through love." Other scientists even charged that IVF would result in horribly deformed children.

In 1971, Edwards and Steptoe received their reply from the British government: their attempts to develop human IVF were considered ethically suspect and unsafe, and they would not receive funding. Undaunted, the two eventually received private money and established Edwards's lab in another hospital near Oldham.

> [Louise Brown] was chubby, full of muscular tone ... I held the head low and we sucked and cleared the mouth and throat. She took a deep breath. Then she yelled and yelled and yelled. I laid her down, all pink and furious, and saw at once that she was externally perfect and beautiful."
> —Patrick Steptoe

The First IVF Baby

Lesley Brown lived in Bristol with her husband, John. After years of trying to conceive, she was discovered to have blocked **fallopian tubes**. Surgery to fix the tubes did not correct her condition. She became depressed, and her doctor finally wrote to Steptoe seeking help. In late 1977, Brown became pregnant through IVF.

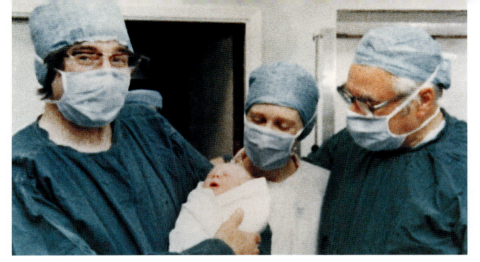

Dr. Robert Edwards holds Louise Brown, the first "test-tube" baby, while Louise's mother, Lesley, and Patrick Steptoe look on.

Lesley Brown's pregnancy was tremendously exciting to Steptoe, Edwards, and the Browns. It was equally exciting to the British media, which soon found out that the controversial experimental procedure might actually be working. The Browns found themselves surrounded by reporters, and Lesley Brown had to be admitted to the Oldham hospital under a false name.

The stress was especially troubling because late in her pregnancy, Brown developed toxemia, a potentially life-threatening condition involving bacteria in the blood. Steptoe was faced with a precarious situation: toxemia could be deadly to the mother, but treatment by inducing birth could be harmful to the baby if it had not developed fully.

Finally on July 25, 1978, Steptoe decided that the time was right for Brown's baby to be born. To avoid reporters, he arranged for a Cesarean section to take place in the middle of the night. At 11:47 p.m., Louise Joy Brown, the world's first baby conceived by IVF, was born.

The Impact of the Solution on Society

Louise Brown was in excellent health (as of 2014, she continues to be well, as is her younger sister, who was also conceived in vitro). Six months later, a second test-tube baby was born, showing that the first success had not been a fluke. Edwards and Steptoe continued to refine their techniques, and in 1987, a year before Steptoe died of cancer, they announced the birth of their thousandth baby fertilized in vitro. By 2014, over five million children were believed to have been conceived and born through IVF worldwide.

Despite its success, IVF remains somewhat controversial. Certain religious groups still condemn the process, considering it unnatural or decrying the discarding of excess embryos. Also, IVF has practical shortcomings: an IVF procedure can be very expensive. Likewise, the success rate is about one in four. Other problems, like birth defects and multiple births, can arise and cause difficulties for mother and child.

For their work, Steptoe and Edwards eventually received awards and accolades. One of the most fundamental was granted in 2010, when Robert Edwards received the Nobel Prize in Physiology and Medicine. Sadly, in 2013, Robert Edwards passed away. Nevertheless, Steptoe and Edwards's work remains as one of the landmarks of twentieth-century medicine. IVF continues to be practiced today, and it offers hope to people who once had none.

Timeline

1913
Patrick Steptoe born in Whitney, England

1925
Robert Edwards born in Leeds, England

1959
Steptoe begins mastering laparoscopic technique

1963
Edwards begins work on fertilizing a human egg

1968
Steptoe and Edwards begin working together

1977
Lesley Brown becomes pregnant through IVF

1978
World's first IVF baby, Louise Joy Brown, is born

1988
Steptoe dies

2013
Edwards dies

Inventor of the Ultraviolet Water Purification System

Ashok Gadgil

1950–

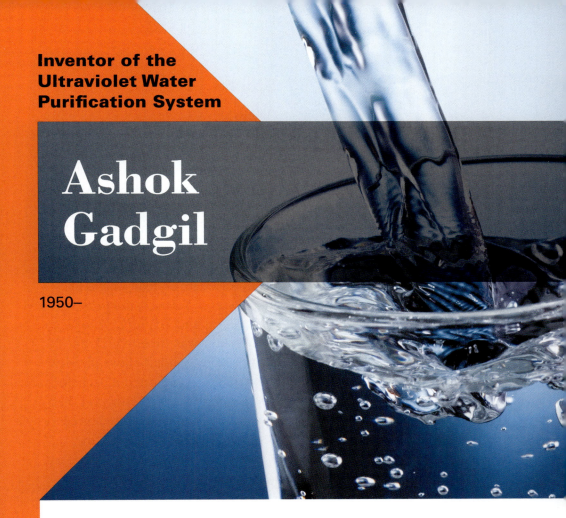

Every day around the world people suffer the consequences of unclean drinking water. Today, as many as 783 million people do not have access to clean, safe water. Efforts have been made for decades to combat polluted water and to give people everywhere the opportunity to drink clean water. One of the main inventions created during the twentieth century was an ultraviolet water purification system. Its inventor, Ashok Gadgil, is one of the leading scientists in the United States and has contributed much time, energy, and dedication to making his product suitable for places all around the world.

Starting Out

Ashok Gadgil poses with his UV Waterworks system.

Ashok Gadgil was born in Bombay, India, in 1950. Like many other children who grew up to be great scientists, he displayed curiosity from an early age about the way things worked. By the time he was in the fourth grade, he had read all of the science textbooks at his local high school. To supplement his knowledge, he read magazines like *Popular Science*, *Popular Mechanics*, and *Scientific American*.

When it was time to pick an area of study, Gadgil chose physics, instead of his parents' preference of medicine. He earned a bachelor's degree in physics at the University of Bombay in 1971. However, he became disenchanted with the theoretical nature of his first degree and decided to pursue a master's degree in applied physics at the Indian Institute of Technology at Kanpur. He graduated in 1973. That year, he traveled to the United States to study at the University of California, Berkeley, where he earned a PhD in 1979 and became an expert on solar energy and heat transfer. In 1980, he began working at the Lawrence Berkeley National Laboratory (LBL), the oldest of the US Department of Energy's national laboratories, as a staff scientist in the energy and environmental technology division.

Defining the Problem

After Gadgil spent three years at LBL, he and his wife moved back to India. Hoping to bring some of the latest ideas in energy, technology, and conservation to his homeland, Gadgil began work at a research institute in New Delhi. He tried to find solutions for basic problems, including the most efficient way to heat water and homes. In five years, he was granted four patents for solar heaters, and he made strides in electrical power conservation. However, growing frustrated by the

Indian government's placing bureaucratic impediments in his path each time he tried to implement a change, he returned to LBL in 1988.

Gadgil's attention was again drawn to India in 1993, when a deadly outbreak of cholera spread throughout the southeastern part of the country. He was reminded of his childhood, when several cousins died from similar waterborne diseases. The quest for safe, clean water became the environmental issue at the forefront of Gadgil's work.

Designing the Solution

The cholera epidemic, which spread from India to Bangladesh and Thailand, killed up to ten thousand people in a matter of months. In addition to the lives lost, the epidemic highlighted a problem that already existed around the world. Waterborne diseases, including cholera, are one of the leading causes of death in many parts of the developing world, particularly sub-Saharan Africa and parts of Asia. An estimated two million people—the vast majority of them children—die from such diseases each year.

Gadgil was deeply affected by the deaths in his homeland. He wanted to develop a cheap, safe, and sturdy water purification system that could operate with little or no energy. The two most common ways of purifying water in the developing world had significant limitations: one method, using chlorine, required training as well as access to chlorine bleach. The other, boiling water, required a great deal of heat, using vital natural resources and causing pollution and deforestation. A third option, using ultraviolet (UV) light, had existed since the end of the nineteenth century, but no practical way for it to be used in poor or rural areas had been developed. Most UV water purification systems required pressurized water, which worked well in areas with reliable supplies of electricity. Poorer areas, however, required a system that could work with little or no electricity.

Gadgil's invention, now known as the UV Waterworks system, is approximately the size of a microwave oven. It could clean water at a rate of 4 gallons (15 liters) per minute and could provide clean, safe drinking water for only pennies per person per year. One unit could serve up to one thousand people for roughly $70 per year. Aside from bringing safe water to countless people around the world, it had an

Gadgil spends much of his time at Lawrence Berkley National Laboratory in San Francisco.

added environmental benefit. If used instead of boiling water, which required burning 2 to 3 tons (1.8 to 2.7 t) of firewood daily, the UV Waterworks system could prevent the production of up to a ton (0.9 t) of carbon dioxide in the air each day.

Applying the Solution

The importance of Gadgil's invention was quickly recognized. In 1996, he received the Discover Award for the most significant environmental invention of the year and the Popular Science award for "Best of What's New—1996." As use of the UV Waterworks expanded, reports of its success started to pour in. In one area in Mexico, for example, the incidence of diarrhea dropped by 93 percent.

Gadgil Expands

Water purification is just one of Gadgil's pursuits as an inventor. He has developed various other safety and environmental devices, including an airvest that keeps toxic fumes away from painters, a space heater suitable for people living in the Himalayas, a water heater for use in cities in India, and a low-environmental-impact energy plant in Brazil. He has been called on to devise ways to protect US citizens in the event of a chemical or biological terrorist attack. He has also helped refugee women in Darfur, Sudan, develop more efficient cooking tools to reduce time spent gathering wood—a time when a woman's risk of assault and rape in war-torn areas is extremely high. Gadgil has also worked to develop a cheap and effective way to remove arsenic, a deadly poison, from the drinking water in Bangladesh.

The Impact of the Solution on Society

Gadgil has been extensively recognized for his tireless work in improving the living conditions of people around the world. In 1991, he was awarded the Pew Fellowship in Conversation and the Environment for his work increasing energy efficiency in developing countries. In 2002, he won the World Technology Award for Energy, and two years later he won the Tech Award Laureate in Health from the Tech Museum of Innovation in San Jose, California.

Today, Gadgil leads a team of scientists at LBL who are particularly concerned with airflow and pollutants. He was one of seven scientists featured in *Me and Isaac Newton*, a full-length documentary about motivation and inspiration, released in 1999 by the noted director Michael Apted. In 2011, he was inducted into the National Academy of Engineering, and in 2012 he won the Lemelson-MIT Award for Global Innovation. Today, he continues his research at Berkeley. His UV Waterworks invention has benefited many people around the globe and will continue to do so for years to come.

Timeline

1950
Ashok Gadgil born in Bombay, India

1979
Gadgil earns a PhD from the University of California, Berkeley

1980
Gadgil begins work at a US Department of Energy laboratory (LBL)

1983
Gadgil returns to India to work at a research institute

1988
Gadgil returns to LBL

1993
Gadgil begins to develop the UV Waterworks system

1996
Gadgil receives several awards for his invention

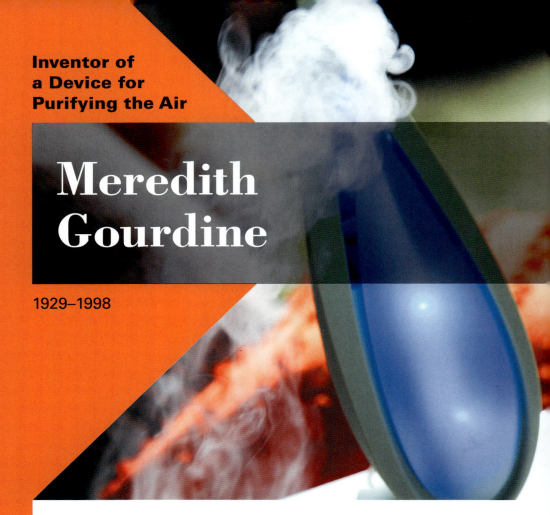

Inventor of a Device for Purifying the Air

Meredith Gourdine

1929–1998

Just as Ashok Gadgil made profound steps in improving the world's water purity, other people have worked hard to make other parts of the environment safe. One such person is Meredith Gourdine, a physicist who invented a technique later used for purifying air inside a home. His life's work helped others, in the US and abroad, and continues to have an impact on modern society.

Beginnings

Meredith Gourdine was born in 1929 in Newark, New Jersey. He grew up in Harlem and then Brooklyn, in New York City. His mother liked math and science, and his father was mechanically inclined. Like many African Americans of that era, however,

Gourdine's parents were unable to obtain an education, and Gourdine's father worked as an automobile mechanic, a painter, and a janitor.

Gourdine's parents encouraged him to become educated. Although he was bright, Gourdine often got bored in class and tended to be a discipline problem. When he was in the seventh grade, a teacher took Gourdine and one of his friends aside and bet them both that they would not be able to pass the math exams to get into Brooklyn Technical High School, a very competitive public school. Gourdine and his friend began studying math after class, first simply to win the bet and then because they found math interesting. They both passed the exam and were admitted. Gourdine did fairly well in math and science at Brooklyn Technical, despite holding down a job with a telegraph company at the same time. He was a good swimmer and eventually was offered a swimming scholarship to the University of Michigan.

Meredith Gourdine, pictured here in 1958

Gourdine decided instead to attend Cornell University in Ithaca, New York, entering in 1948. It was a risky decision because Gourdine had no scholarship to Cornell. He had only the money he had saved from his high school job, which was enough to pay for a single semester.

The Olympics

Gourdine wanted to study engineering physics at Cornell, but the program was extremely competitive, and his grades in high school were not good enough to gain him entrance. "That made me kind of furious," he later recalled. As a result, he worked extremely hard his first semester at Cornell, earning the grades required to transfer into the engineering physics program. His top grades also earned him a scholarship for the rest of his time at Cornell.

Meredith Gourdine (*right*) poses with fellow medalists Jerry Biffle (*left*) and Oedoen Foeldesi (*center*) at the Olympic Games in Helsinki, Finland, in 1952.

Gourdine also kept up with his athletics, joining Cornell's track-and-field team. He proved an exceptional athlete, winning numerous intercollegiate titles. In 1952, Gourdine competed in the Olympic Games, which were held in Helsinki, Finland. Gourdine won the silver medal in the long jump.

Gourdine completed his studies at Cornell in 1953 and joined the US Navy. The navy bored Gourdine, however, and he decided to return to school. He applied for a Guggenheim Fellowship to study at the Jet Propulsion Laboratory (JPL) in Pasadena, California, which is managed by the California Institute of Technology; he won the fellowship in 1955.

Finding a Field

Gourdine received his engineering doctorate in 1960. While at JPL, Gourdine focused on the rather obscure field of **electrogasdynamics**.

One aspect of particular interest to Gourdine was a phenomenon that scientists had known about for centuries: moving, ionized gas can produce electricity, although too little to be of practical use. Gourdine thought he might be able to figure out a way to increase the amount of electricity this phenomenon produced, perhaps enough to create a practical electrical generator. Gourdine hit upon the idea of forcing the ionized gas through a very narrow channel. The channel lay in an electrical field, and the interaction of the field and the ions converted their **kinetic energy** into electricity.

The device developed by Gourdine greatly increased the amount of electricity generated by flowing gas. Gourdine was disappointed by the reaction of his supervisor at JPL, who merely complimented Gourdine on his work; no attempt was made to develop the idea, and no effort was begun to find out if a practical electrical generator could be made to use the increased electricity. Although Gourdine enjoyed working at JPL, the reaction of his supervisor made him realize that an academic career was a dead end for him. The experience convinced Gourdine that he was never going to accomplish anything meaningful at the laboratory.

Managing Himself

Gourdine decided that the private sector held more promise. Although he considered starting his own company, he had a family to support. Consequently, he took a job with the Plasmodyne Corporation and then with the Curtiss-Wright Corporation. Gourdine was unsuccessful in his attempts to interest his employers and other companies in his generator idea. In 1964, Gourdine borrowed money from friends and established his own company, Gourdine Systems, based in Livingston, New Jersey. Nine years later, he established a second company, Energy Innovations, in Houston, Texas.

Establishing his own firms allowed Gourdine to invent full-time. The next few decades were a period of remarkable creativity, and he was granted some forty US patents between 1969 and 1996. The patents covered a wide array of applications, including reproducing images, detecting dust, cooling computer chips, and clearing fog from airport runways—all of which stemmed from his understanding of the behavior of ions.

Not all of Gourdine's ideas resulted in marketable products, however. Despite years of effort, including presenting the technology

> "I was always doing things people said couldn't be done ... That's the way I operated. If somebody said it couldn't be done, that's what I would try to do."
> —Meredith Gourdine

before a committee of the US Senate in 1967, Gourdine was never able to market his electrical generator for large-scale use. Instead, he sold small models of his generators to schools and laboratories interested in studying electrogasdynamics.

Other ideas were more successful. In the late 1960s, Gourdine developed a new technology for painting metal that was widely adopted in factories. Gourdine's system was used for many years before it was replaced by newer technology.

Defining the Problem

In the 1960s, Gourdine became very interested in the problem of air pollution. During that time, the quality of air was becoming progressively worse due to such harmful elements as gasoline and insecticides. In 1966, Gourdine served on a task force examining air

A Focus on Paint

Gourdine's focus on the behavior of electrically charged particles resulted in the development of a new way to paint metal products such as cars, refrigerators, and other machinery. Painting such products is not simply a cosmetic issue: unpainted metals will rust when exposed to moisture. Previously, workers in an automobile factory would spray liquid paint onto a car. Spots would be missed, particularly if the body of the car had many hard-to-reach crevices. Once the car left the factory and became exposed to rain and grime, the missed spots would rust, shortening the vehicle's life.

Gourdine's system, in contrast, used dry-powder paint. The powder was given a positive electrical charge, and the automobile was given a negative electrical charge, creating a magnetic attraction between the two.

When the powdered paint was blown onto the metal, it clung to the object. Bare spots of metal had a greater attraction to excess paint powder than spots already covered with powder, so the paint powder got into every crevice. The painted object was then baked to melt the powdered paint and give it a smooth finish.

pollution in New York City, which determined that the city had unsafe air, in large part because of the widespread use of incinerators that burned garbage.

Incinerator smoke contained **noxious** particles that were too small to be removed with a conventional filter. More advanced filtration systems were available, but they were large and very expensive. In addition, these systems typically cleaned smoke by running it through water, resulting in large quantities of wastewater.

Designing the Solution

In the early 1970s, Gourdine developed an effective filtering device that was far smaller than existing systems. The filter worked by applying a negative charge to the particles in smoke. Once those particles were negatively charged, they passed by a positively charged metal plate. The smoke particles clung to the plate, which could then be cleaned or replaced. Gourdine's device was approved for use in New Jersey and was used on a test basis in New York City later in the 1970s. Although the filter worked well, eventually incinerators themselves fell out of favor and were banned in urban areas.

Applying the Solution

While Gourdine's air-filtration technology was never widely used for incinerators, it was used elsewhere, in particular for in-home air purifiers. Home air purifiers are small enough to be picked up and moved from room to room, and they have become popular in the United States because of concerns about indoor air pollution. Mold spores and solvent fumes released by carpets and upholstery, as well as concerns about increased rates of childhood asthma, have led to the widespread popularity of home air purifiers. These devices clear the home of such harmful elements, making the air easier to breathe and less polluted.

The Impact of the Solution on Society

Following the ban on incinerators, Gourdine continued working throughout the 1980s and 1990s. In his last years, he suffered significant health problems, including diabetes, which caused him to lose his sight and a leg. He died in Houston, Texas, in November 1998, at the age of sixty-nine.

Gourdine's original intent for his invention may have been completely different from the final created product, but his work and its effects on society have profoundly changed the way pollutants are filtered through the air. Major companies such as Honeywell, Sears, and Panasonic sell air purifiers today; many of these purifiers use the ionizing technology developed by Gourdine. This testifies to Gourdine's place as a remarkable inventor in health and medical technology.

Timeline

1929
Meredith Gourdine born in Newark, New Jersey

1952
Gourdine wins a silver medal at the Helsinki Olympic Games

1960
Gourdine receives a doctorate from the California Institute of Technology

1964
Gourdine founds Gourdine Systems

1966
Gourdine examines air pollution in New York City

Early 1970s
Gourdine develops a new air filtering system

1973
Gourdine establishes Energy Innovations

1998
Gourdine dies

Inventor of the Pacemaker

Wilson Greatbatch

1919–2011

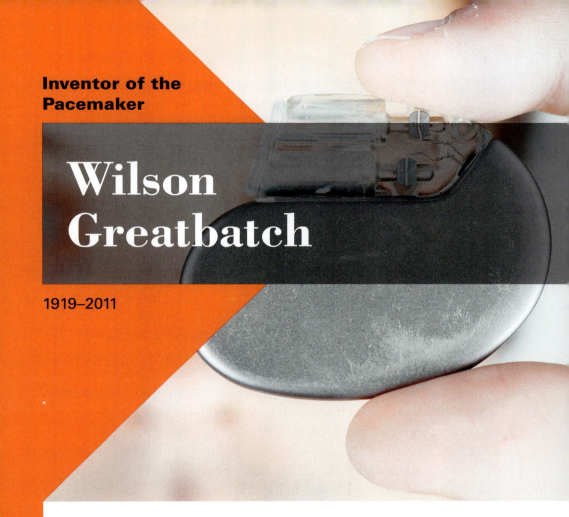

Wilson Greatbatch was an engineer and inventor who held more than 325 patents. However, the invention he is probably best known for is the pacemaker, an artificial electrical device that is placed in the chest to help control heart rhythms in cardiac patients who have **arrhythmias**. The pacemaker helps the patient's heart beat at a normal rate. Arrhythmias can be dangerous or fatal; Greatbatch's device was a revolutionary treatment when he introduced it in the late 1950s, and it is still in use today.

Growing Up Greatbatch

Wilson Greatbatch was born on September 6, 1919, in the steel town of Buffalo, New York. His father, Warren Greatbatch, was an

Wilson Greatbatch poses in his workshop in 1997.

English immigrant who worked as a construction contractor. His mother, Charlotte (Recktenwalt) Greatbatch, a secretary, was Warren's second wife; his first wife and the mother of Wilson's half-brother, Neville, had died. Warren and Charlotte Greatbatch named their only child together Wilson, in honor of President Woodrow Wilson.

Young Wilson Greatbatch was fascinated by radio technology. He and his friends were Boy Scouts and later moved on to the Sea Scouts program, which had a base on the Niagara River. It was there that Wilson and his friends convinced the Scout headquarters to give them a loft where they could build a radio transmitter. Their transmitter worked so well that one night in 1936, during a big hurricane, Greatbatch heard on the receiver traffic coming from New England. He went on the air and relayed messages back and forth so that people could bring blankets and food to those in need. Greatbatch and his friends got a citation from the American Red Cross for their aid that night. He and his fellow Sea Scouts later trained younger Scouts in radio transmission and helped them get their amateur radio licenses.

After high school, Greatbatch began his studies at Buffalo State Teachers College and served in the Navy Reserve, but when the United States entered World War II, he left his studies and went into active duty, where he worked on shipboard communications and guidance systems. Greatbatch was later transferred into something "new and secret" during his navy time—radar. He was trained in this new technology and then helped set up a radio school in Annapolis, Maryland, where he was an instructor. He was then transferred to Corpus Christi, Texas, where he became a flight instructor for radar patrols. He later flew combat missions for the navy as a dive bomber, where one of his shipmates was Gerald Ford, who later became president of the United States.

After his navy service, Greatbatch received an honorable discharge in 1945. He returned home and worked as a telephone repairman for a year before he entered Cornell University. By this point he had married his childhood sweetheart, Eleanor Wright, and started a family with her.

The Greatbatches had five children: a daughter, Anne, and four sons, Warren, Kenneth, John, and Peter. Greatbatch worked several jobs to support his growing family while he attended Cornell, ultimately earning his bachelor's degree in electrical engineering in 1950 and his master's degree in electrical engineering from the University of Buffalo in 1957, after which he became manager of the electronics division at Taber Instrument Corporation. He worked for Taber until he conceived of the idea of the pacemaker, which Taber was unwilling to pursue. At that point, Greatbatch became an independent inventor and entrepreneur.

A Working Man

Because Greatbatch had a growing family while he was attending college, he had to work numerous jobs while completing his studies. As a result, his grades weren't outstanding. However, he gained a lot of experience while going to school and working—he ran a radio transmitter, helped build radio telescope equipment that was sent to Puerto Rico, participated in conditioned reflex experiments, and built amplifiers to monitor animals' vital signs for Cornell's prestigious center for Pavlovian psychology. These last two experiences enabled him to later build amplifiers for one of the first chimpanzees sent into space and got Greatbatch into the field of medical electronics. In fact, Greatbatch and a few of his Cornell classmates were instrumental in starting Cornell's chapter of the Biomedical Engineering Group, which was the first local chapter of the IEEE (Institute of Electrical and Electronics Engineers).

Defining the Problem

During Wilson Greatbatch's Cornell days, one of his jobs was building amplifiers to monitor animal vital signs. Specifically, some of his work was building amplifiers for EKGs (electrocardiograms). While Greatbatch was doing this work, he met with surgeons from Boston who had come to do experimental brain surgery on some of the department's goats. During their lunch breaks, the surgeons and Greatbatch would sit outside and talk. In these talks, Greatbatch learned about a cardiac condition known as complete heart block. That is when a nerve in the heart stops functioning, and the auricle and ventricle of the heart no longer beat in the correct rhythm with each other. Sometimes the ventricle stops beating completely, which causes people to faint. In the 1950s, 50 percent of the people suffering from complete heart block died within a year of diagnosis.

Greatbatch saw complete heart block as a communications problem. As a communications engineer, he felt there was a solution to this. His early thoughts on the matter were about something like an external pacemaker—that if one could connect wires to the heart and send an electrical signal through them, it could simulate one beat of the heart. However, here logistics became a problem—it wasn't feasible for someone to have to artificially stimulate his or her heart for each beat.

Around this same time, external pacemakers were invented—much like what Greatbatch first envisioned—but the patient had to remain plugged into a TV-sized box for the rest of his or her life. It was a solution, but not a terrific one, and Greatbatch wanted to do better. He wanted to find a way to build a much smaller device that could be implanted in a patient's body. The technology wasn't yet available at this point—engineers were still working with large vacuum tubes, which weren't small enough to be useful in this context.

Designing the Solution

Since the technology wasn't initially available to create the internal pacemaker, Greatbatch put the idea in the back of his mind for several years. However, when, in the mid-1950s, transistors were introduced, Greatbatch realized the time was right.

In 1956, he was working as an assistant professor in electrical engineering at the University at Buffalo. He was building an oscillator to record heart rhythms for the Chronic Disease Research Institute, and he accidently installed the wrong size resistor in the device. However, he discovered that the resulting electronic device produced a series of intermittent electrical pulses, which made him think of a heartbeat and reminded him of his idea of the pacemaker.

This happy accident made Greatbatch reflect on his earlier ideas. He set to work designing a small, implantable pacemaker that could be kept safe from bodily fluids. As it turned out, Greatbatch wasn't the only researcher trying to create an implant for humans. In fact, he was in a race with other researchers in the United States and in Sweden. Greatbatch was determined to perfect his device before the other researchers did.

A heart patient displays her pacemaker in 1961.

By May 7, 1958, he had a prototype that could control a dog's heartbeat, and doctors—including one of Greatbatch's two eventual collaborators, Dr. William C. Chardack—at the Veterans Administration hospital in Buffalo demonstrated it. This was the first time Greatbatch had really found any interest in his device. Dr. Chardack recognized that if the device worked, it could save ten thousand lives a year. Greatbatch hadn't been able to interest any other doctors he approached—they all saw complete heart block as an incurable disease and didn't feel it was worth wasting research time on.

Upon the initial success of Greatbatch's prototype, he realized he needed to make some refinements, but there was definite potential in his device. He also realized that he could build the pacemakers himself. Greatbatch quit his jobs and began working full-time building pacemakers in his backyard barn. In the next two years, he built fifty pacemakers. During this time, he relied on his large vegetable garden to help feed his family, as well as the $2,000 he had in savings. He enlisted his wife, Eleanor, to help him administer shock tests as he worked on the device.

Applying the Solution

Wilson Greatbatch achieved his goal of being the first researcher to invent a practical, usable device to correct arrhythmia in cardiac patients. Just two years after his device was demonstrated on dogs at the Veterans Administration hospital, Greatbatch's device had been refined and improved, and it had been implanted in ten human patients, two of whom were children. The first pacemaker implanted in a human was placed in the chest of a seventy-seven-year-old man, who ultimately lived eighteen months with it.

In 1961, Greatbatch licensed the device to Medtronic, a Minneapolis company that had developed an external pacemaker but not yet an internal one. Medtronic later became the world leader in cardiac stimulation and defibrillation, thanks in part to its licensing Greatbatch's invention and taking him on as part of its board of directors. Medtronic was technically bankrupt in 1961, but Greatbatch encouraged the company to discontinue some of its less successful products and focus on the pacemaker. Within two years the company was number one in the industry.

Greatbatch's licensing of the pacemaker to Medtronic didn't stop his work on the device. Early on, Greatbatch recognized that the mercury batteries used in pacemakers had limitations. The battery manufacturer insisted that the batteries would run six years, but Greatbatch and Medtronic found that the batteries actually rarely lasted longer than two years. The average patient receiving a pacemaker lived six years after receiving his first pacemaker, so the two-year life of the batteries meant that the average patient went through three pacemakers during his final years of life! Greatbatch recognized that if he could create a battery that lasted ten years, then most patients would only ever need one pacemaker in their lifetime. The only problem was their battery supplier, Mallory, wasn't interested in creating a new type of battery.

So Greatbatch approached Medtronic and suggested that it create the new battery itself. When the head of Medtronic declined, Greatbatch canceled his contract with the company and sold it his patents. The split was amicable, and Greatbatch moved away from designing pacemakers and into designing batteries.

Greatbatch first considered rechargeable batteries but quickly realized that the quality of rechargeable batteries was not good enough to use. He then tried nuclear batteries using plutonium-239, and those were extremely effective but had a lot of drawbacks. Finally, he found another solution: lithium. He heard about lithium batteries in 1970 and found that they had a much longer life than mercury batteries and were far less troublesome than plutonium batteries. In fact, one of the first patients to receive a pacemaker with a lithium battery was an Australian who went out into the outback and away from civilization. When they finally caught up with him in the early 1990s, they discovered that his lithium-powered pacemaker had been running for twenty-two years!

When Greatbatch came up with the idea that lithium batteries could be used in implantable pacemakers, he originally intended to have another company produce the batteries, and he would seal them for use in pacemakers. However, the factory for the Catalyst Research Corporation, which had agreed to manufacture the batteries, experienced a flood from a nearby stream, and the floodwater mixed with the lithium and sodium used in the batteries and blew up the factory.

Greatbatch was left with no choice but to produce batteries himself, and the resulting company, Wilson Greatbatch Ltd., eventually grew to supply 90 percent of the world's pacemaker batteries.

The Impact of the Solution on Society

Since its invention, the implantable pacemaker has saved millions of lives. According to the American Heart Association, more than half a million pacemakers are implanted every year. The device has been refined over the years, but it remains an incredibly reliable treatment for heart patients, especially when Greatbatch improved the batteries used in the device. Astonishingly, it took only five years from its formal 1960 introduction for the pacemaker to become the universally accepted treatment for complete heart block. In the medical industry, where treatments are typically slowly phased in, this quick adoption of a treatment was almost unheard of.

In 1985, the National Society of Professional Engineers named the pacemaker one of the ten greatest engineering achievements of the last fifty years. In 1986, Wilson Greatbatch was inducted into the Inventors Hall of Fame, and in 2003 the National Academy of Engineering, of which Greatbatch was a member, cited his pacemaker as one of the greatest engineering achievements of the twentieth century. In 1990, President George H.W. Bush presented Greatbatch with the National Medal of Technology, and Greatbatch also received the prestigious Lemelson-MIT Prize. He died in 2011 at the age of ninety-two.

Timeline

1919
Wilson Greatbatch born in Buffalo, New York

1945
Greatbatch is honorably discharged from the US Navy

1950
Greatbatch earns his bachelor's degree from Cornell University

1956
Greatbatch inadvertently creates a device that is the basis for his implantable pacemaker

1958
Greatbatch's prototype for the implantable pacemaker is tested at the VA hospital in Buffalo, NY

1960
The first pacemakers are implanted in humans and met with success

1961
Greatbatch licenses his invention to Medtronic, which becomes the leader in cardiac devices

1970
Greatbatch designs the lithium battery for use in pacemakers, which drastically extends the device's life

2011
Greatbatch dies

Inventor of Various Scientific Instruments

Robert Hooke

1635–1703

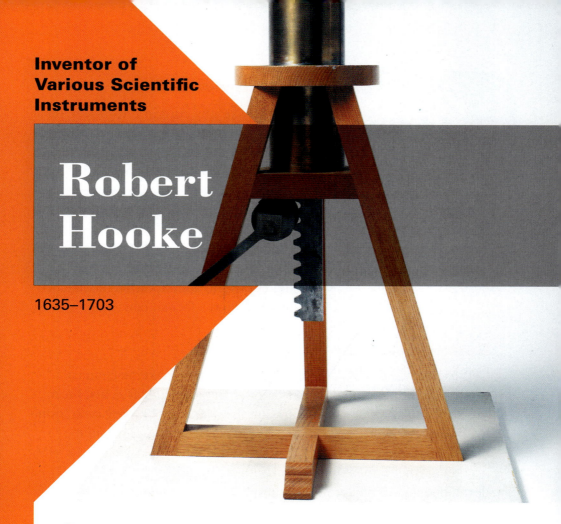

Some inventors focus their entire careers on inventing one mechanism or technique, while others invent many things in their lifetime. One inventor who has gained more recognition in recent years for his many inventions is Robert Hooke. He was a contemporary of Isaac Newton (1643–1727), and while during his life he achieved many "firsts," he remained relatively unknown for decades following his death. This partly had to do with rivalry between him and Newton and their debate concerning which of them invented certain devices first. Nonetheless, Robert Hooke is now known for many of his scientific inventions, which changed the way the world operated.

An illustration of Robert Hooke with a wheel barometer

Hooke Grows Up

Robert Hooke was born in Freshwater, on the Isle of Wight, near England, on July 18, 1635. His father, the parish curate Reverend John Hooke, intended his son to follow him in a career in the church. However, the young Hooke suffered ill health for much of his childhood. Frequent headaches plagued him, making reading difficult. As a result, John Hooke believed that his son would not live to adulthood and abandoned plans for Robert's formal education.

Defining the Problem

Left to his own devices, Robert Hooke began to make mechanical toys while developing his observational and mechanical skills. From his own study of his surroundings on the island, Hooke began to form his belief that nature operated as a complex machine. He tried to understand as many aspects of this vast machine as possible.

According to the author John Aubrey (1626–1697), Hooke had developed a strong interest in painting when the painter John Hoskins came to Freshwater to draw. Not yet in his teens, Hooke decided he would learn to draw and paint, and he started to sketch. In 1648, upon the death of his father, Hooke went to London with his inheritance of £100 to study with the celebrated painter Peter Lely (1618–1680). The money was meant for Lely, but Hooke soon determined that he could pursue his goals without the help of Lely and so withdrew from Lely's tutelage. The thirteen-year-old Hooke decided instead to enter Westminster School.

At Westminster, Hooke studied Greek and Latin, learned to play the organ, and, according to Aubrey, "in one week's time made himself master of the first six books of Euclid"—a reference to the writings of the great Greek mathematician. Hooke's talents for geometry and mechanics advanced rapidly at Westminster, and in 1653 Hooke entered Christ College of Oxford University. There he studied with many prominent scientists of his time, including the chemist Robert Boyle (1627–1691), with whom Hooke worked especially closely.

Designing the Solution

Beginning in 1655, Hooke was employed to assist Boyle in his work. He would remain with Boyle until 1662; during this period Hooke made the first in a long line of inventions. Boyle, noticing Hooke's talent for designing and modifying various scientific instruments, asked his assistant to construct an air pump for him to use in determining the laws of gases. The air pump Hooke made was a vast improvement over others then in use and is effectively the same design in use for manual air pumps today.

Also while working under Boyle, Hooke formulated what would become known as Hooke's law. This law states that an elastic material, such as a spring, will stretch to a degree proportional to the stress exerted on it. This concept, which Hooke used to design a more accurate system of balance springs in watches, among other applications, would remain important in the field of structural engineering into the twenty-first century.

Applying the Solution

As an indirect result of Boyle's patronage, Hooke was elected to the prestigious post of curator of experiments at the newly founded Royal Society in 1662. In this capacity, Hooke was responsible for supervising all experiments performed at the society's meetings, which featured many prominent scientists. Here Hooke's already abundant range of scientific interests found an even broader arena as dozens of others brought their interests and research to the society's halls.

While Hooke was curator of experiments, his mechanical skills led to his inventing dozens of new devices, as well as improving the inventions of others. Prominent among these was a reflecting microscope, which surpassed anything that had been constructed to date. Other important inventions from this period include a reflecting telescope, an improved barometer (Hooke was perhaps the first person to associate the drop in barometric pressure with the approach of a storm), the universal joint (sometimes called the Hooke joint), and a simple calculating machine. His experiments demonstrated in rough outline the laws of gravity several years before Newton formulated these laws in more polished form, and Hooke proposed a theory ("inverse-square relationship") to express the decrease of gravity as an object reached a greater and greater distance from Earth. He also at this time proposed in rudimentary form a wave theory of light, a dynamical theory of heat, and even an evolutionary theory based on his close study of fossils using his new microscope.

The Impact of the Solution on Society

The most important result of all these far-reaching inquiries was Hooke's *Micrographia*, published in 1665. In this work, Hooke

London's Great Fire

The Great Fire of 1666 caused enormous damage to the city of London. Although relatively few people died in the fire (figures range from five to twenty), buildings across more than 400 acres (161 hectares) were destroyed. The fire burned for four days, and when it was over, the government was faced with the prospect of rebuilding.

Robert Hooke was named surveyor of the city of London and put in charge of laying out the overall plan for reconstruction. Christopher Wren (1632–1723), one of England's greatest architects, was responsible for designing specific buildings. As assistant to Wren, Hooke also participated in the design of a number of important buildings, including the Monument to the Great Fire, which stands on Fish Street Hill, near where the fire started. Because the two men worked very closely together, determining which of them can be credited with specific concepts or work remains difficult.

Hooke was specifically charged with laying out the street plan for the new London. He proposed a design that included a grid pattern featuring wide boulevards with smaller arteries coming off them. The wrote about his findings on a broad range of phenomena, mostly observations he made with his microscope. Accompanying Hooke's text were many fascinating, often quite beautiful, drawings Hooke himself made of the objects he observed through his microscope. Hooke's *Micrographia* effectively began the field of microbiology; in fact, Hooke coined the term "cell" in this work to describe the structures he observed first in cork and then in plants. These minute, honeycomb-like structures reminded him of monks' quarters (*cellula* in Latin). Hooke is also credited with starting the science of crystals; he was the first to explain the complex structure of crystals, including that of snowflakes, in *Micrographia*.

In 1665, Hooke became professor of geometry at Gresham College in London, a position he held for thirty years. However, the following year a fire devastated much of the city. The Great Fire of 1666 left many of the city's buildings and neighborhoods in ruins. Hooke was named surveyor of the city of London after the fire and became many property disputes that arose after the damage, however, made Hooke's plan impossible to implement. In fact, he often had to serve as **arbitrator** between people who were arguing over property lines. London streets were, as a result, rebuilt according to the original medieval design. Many today blame the congestion in London on the property disputes that followed the Great Fire and prevented Hooke's plan from being adopted.

This painting shows the destruction of London in 1666.

Robert Hooke

chief assistant to the great architect Christopher Wren (1632–1723) in various rebuilding projects. Although his expertise was primarily in mechanical and engineering matters, Hooke also proved himself to be a skilled designer and architect. Among his designs were the Bethlem Royal Hospital (also called "Bedlam," one of the first psychiatric hospitals) as well as the Royal College of Physicians. He also designed, with Wren, the Monument to the Great Fire, which stands near the north end of London Bridge, not far from where the fire began.

Up until his death in March 1703, Robert Hooke remained an active member of society, delivering addresses to the Royal Society and inventing numerous other devices, such as a type of odometer; an "otocousticon," which is a prototype of a hearing aid; and a telescope that could be used underwater. His genius and determination continued until his final days; however, overshadowed by the success of Sir Isaac Newton, his contributions faded into obscurity after he died. Only recently were his achievements recognized and Hooke uplifted as a significant inventor of the seventeenth century.

Timeline

1635
Robert Hooke born on the Isle of Wight

1648
Hooke travels to London to study painting

1655
Hooke goes to work assisting chemist Robert Boyle

1662
Hooke becomes curator of experiments of the Royal Society

1665
Hooke publishes *Micrographia*

1666
Hooke becomes surveyor of the city of London after the Great Fire

1703
Hooke dies

Inventor of the Smallpox Vaccine

Edward Jenner

1749–1823

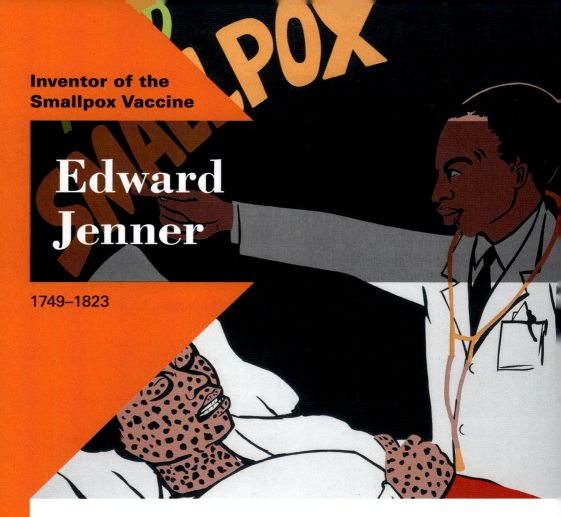

Since the first diseases raced across humanity, people had searched for ways to combat them. Many potential remedies came and went throughout the centuries. However, it was not until the eighteenth century that a lasting solution was invented. Among the most devastating illnesses was smallpox. It was smallpox that would eventually earn a place in history as the only disease to be defeated by human efforts. Likewise, this disease would prove the key to unlocking a powerful remedy against many diseases: vaccination. The man to develop the vaccine was Edward Jenner, the hero in this war against destructive diseases.

Jenner's Origins

Edward Jenner was born May 17, 1749, in Berkeley, Gloucestershire, in the southwest of England. Growing up in this rural environment, Jenner became a very close observer of the natural world around him. His formal schooling began at Wooten-under-Edge in Gloucestershire, then continued at Cirencester. At age thirteen he was apprenticed to a doctor named Daniel Ludlow. In 1770, Jenner went to London to study under the renowned surgeon, anatomist, and naturalist John Hunter at St. George's Hospital. Hunter chose Jenner partly on the basis of the young man's keen interest in botany and zoology, in addition to his medical talents. Jenner studied and worked with Hunter for three years before returning to his native Berkeley in 1773 to establish a practice as a country doctor. He remained in Berkeley, working as a doctor and naturalist, for the remainder of his life.

Edward Jenner transformed medicine with his invention of the smallpox vaccine.

John Hunter had encouraged Jenner's natural curiosity, urging his bright young pupil to take an imaginative and experimental approach to medicine (while still observing the day's standard medical principles). Jenner soon found occasion to apply his imaginative and observational powers to a question that had long occupied naturalists. He gained the notice of the scientific community by providing an explanation for the strange nesting habits of the cuckoo, which lays its eggs in another bird's nest, expelling the host bird's own young.

Jenner's paper detailing his observations of the cuckoo won him election into the prestigious Royal Society in 1789. However, his reputation rests on other work of far greater importance. Jenner's experiments stemming from his observation of the relationship between cowpox and smallpox led him to develop the vaccine that would eventually lead to the elimination of smallpox throughout the world.

Defining the Problem

By the time Jenner began to study smallpox, the disease had already plagued humans for centuries. It had first begun in China, then spread throughout Europe in the sixteenth and seventeenth centuries. Eventually, it was carried to the Americas during the "voyages of discovery," where the Spanish, English, and other European nations established the first European settlements amongst the Native people. There, it killed more of the indigenous populations than did all the battles with European settlers.

In Jenner's time, smallpox accounted for one-third of all children's deaths in Europe, and it devastated populations around the globe. Caused by the virus *variola*, which enters the body through the lungs and then spreads through the blood to infect the internal organs, smallpox becomes evident when it erupts as small pink spots that grow to become raised, open blisters.

There are two versions of the disease—*variola major* and *variola minor*. Each version produces the same recognizable spots, or pox, but hits its victims differently. *Variola major* causes severe effects, whereas *variola minor* brings on a light case. In depicting the disease here, it will be classified simply as smallpox.

The Chinese had developed a method of providing immunity against smallpox by blowing flakes from a smallpox scab up the nostrils of healthy people. This process was called inoculation. Later, a woman named Lady Mary Wortley Montagu, who had been affected previously by smallpox, observed this practice in Turkey in the early 1700s and introduced it to England in the 1720s. Inoculation proved effective in some cases, but it was still very dangerous. Many people treated in this manner developed full-blown smallpox.

Around Jenner's time, inoculation was used by doctors in Turkey and Greece; they had discovered that injecting some of the pus from small pox blisters into a healthy body could produce a mild case

Jenner and the Cuckoo

Although Edward Jenner is best known for his development of a vaccine to immunize people against smallpox, his interests were wide-ranging. He made important contributions to the field of natural history as well as medicine. The first of these was a paper in which he explained the bizarre nesting habits of the cuckoo, a bird that had puzzled observers for centuries.

An adult female cuckoo will lay a single egg in the nest of a bird from another species, usually that of a hedge sparrow. The host bird's own eggs and **fledglings** are removed from the nest, and the cuckoo fledgling is left alone to receive the care of the foster parent. Scientists always believed that the adult cuckoo was responsible for clearing the nest prior to laying its one egg there.

Jenner hypothesized that, in fact, the newly hatched cuckoo fledgling, not the parent, pushed the eggs or young sparrows out of the host bird's nest. One of his findings was that the young cuckoo's body had a unique depression in its back, between its wings, with which it could cup objects and push them backward. This depression disappears by the time the fledgling cuckoo is twelve days old. Jenner conducted many experiments to support his hypothesis before presenting his findings in 1788 to the Royal Society, which made him a fellow the following year for his contribution.

Jenner's hypothesis remained open to question until the twentieth century, when naturalists developed the means of photographing the fledglings in action, proving that Jenner was right.

of the disease but would leave the body immune afterward. This version of inoculation also was very risky. Nevertheless, it became widespread in England by the eighteenth century, as fears of the disease led people to take extreme measures.

Designing the Solution

Jenner himself had been inoculated as a boy and suffered badly as a result. He vowed to eradicate the disease. He became interested in reports that milkmaids who had been exposed to cowpox appeared to be immune to smallpox. After years of observing people who had contracted cowpox and theorizing that there was a connection, Jenner decided to carry out a formal experiment. In May 1796, he extracted fluid from an open cowpox mark on the hand of a milkmaid named Sarah Nelmes and used it to inoculate James Phipps, an eight-year-old boy who had agreed to be involved. As Jenner expected, the boy developed cowpox. Then, six weeks later, he inoculated Phipps with smallpox. To his great relief, Jenner saw that the boy did not develop smallpox. A short time later, he introduced smallpox again on Phipps's skin, and again no infection developed. Jenner tentatively concluded that his theory was correct, reasoning that immunity to smallpox could be achieved much more safely by injecting cowpox material into the bodies of uninfected people.

Jenner named his procedure "vaccination," borrowing the Latin name for cow, *vacca*, and deriving from it *vaccinia*, or "cowpox." Then in 1798 he published the results of his smallpox research in a paper, which he called "An Inquiry into the Causes and Effects of the *Variolae Vaccinae*."

Jenner continued to carry out research and publish his accounts over the next two years. All the evidence confirmed Jenner's initial theories about immunization. However, as with any new invention, there were people who looked at his findings with scrutiny.

Applying the Solution

Jenner's technique for preventing smallpox faced various kinds of opposition. One of these was from the medical community itself: many doctors had established successful businesses by becoming "inoculators"—those who practiced the risky procedure of injecting people with the smallpox virus. Jenner's much safer and more effective treatment threatened these doctors' incomes. Superstition spawned opposition from other quarters: some people feared being treated with materials taken from "God's lowlier creatures."

Even those medical practitioners who supported Jenner's findings faced difficulty incorporating his practices. Cowpox was not nearly as widely occurring as smallpox, and doctors often had to obtain samples of cowpox directly from Jenner. Since the people handling these samples usually were the same people handling smallpox, cowpox samples often became contaminated with smallpox. As a result, many people thought that infection with or vaccination with cowpox was no safer than exposure to smallpox.

Even so, Jenner's vaccination methods eventually won widespread favor. The British government recognized his work in 1800. By that year more than one hundred thousand people worldwide had received Jenner's vaccine. Demand increased so quickly that Jenner had to develop a means of transporting the vaccine long distances. This he did by drying vaccination material so that it could be stored in a glass tube for up to three months.

The Impact of the Solution on Society

Jenner spent the remainder of his life as consultant and supplier of his vaccine to doctors around the world. He once referred to himself as "the Vaccine Clerk to the World." Although Jenner did not patent his vaccine, preferring to make it as widely available as possible, the British government awarded him £10,000 in 1802 and another £20,000 in 1807 as compensation for his valuable efforts on behalf of humanity.

> "The annihilation of the Small Pox, the most dreadful scourge of the human species, must be the final result of [my] practice."
> —Edward Jenner

Jenner was honored by Napoleon Bonaparte in France, and, in the United States, Thomas Jefferson requested the vaccine from Jenner to vaccinate his family and neighbors at Monticello. In London, Jenner formed a society to promote the use of his vaccine to eradicate smallpox around the world. This organization became known as the National Vaccine Establishment in 1808. In 1821, Jenner was appointed "physician extraordinary" to King George IV.

Despite the accolades, Jenner remained in his native Gloucestershire, corresponding about the progress of his vaccination around the world, collecting fossils, and propagating hybrid plants in

World Health Organization headquarters

his garden. In addition to his seminal work developing the cowpox vaccine, Jenner also made pioneering observations into heart disease. He performed several postmortem examinations on bodies of patients who had died complaining of chest pain—or angina pectoris. Jenner noted that the arteries around these patients' hearts had hardened and were blocked with fatty deposits. His observations advanced the practices of doctors treating heart disease. Jenner died of a stroke on January 26, 1823, at age seventy-three.

In Jenner's native England, smallpox vaccination was made compulsory in 1853. Even so, smallpox outbreaks continued there into the 1960s, mainly after travelers returned from other countries where the disease still existed. In 1967, the World Health Organization (WHO) launched an aggressive worldwide campaign to end smallpox. That year the WHO estimated that some fifteen million cases occurred each year, mainly in Africa, India, and South America. After thirteen years of chasing down outbreaks in these areas, in 1980 the WHO finally declared, "Smallpox Is Dead!" At the turn of the twenty-first century, the last remaining specimens of the disease were held under extremely close security in laboratories in the United States and Siberia—or so it was thought until July 2014, when several undocumented vials of smallpox were found in a disease control center warehouse.

Edward Jenner's work remains a tremendous benefit to humanity. It eventually led to the eradication of one of the deadliest disease to attack humans. His explorations into new areas of medicine, and his pioneering efforts to eliminate the disease entirely from society, are uplifted as remarkable achievements in the modern age. It is thanks to Jenner that so many people are in this world today, for without this discovery, humanity's survival rate could have been gravely affected.

Timeline

1749
Edward Jenner born in Gloucestershire, England

1773
Jenner completes his medical training

1796
Jenner conducts his first successful smallpox vaccination

1798
Jenner publishes "An Inquiry into the Causes and Effects of the Variolae Vaccinae"

1808
Jenner forms the National Vaccine Establishment

1821
Jenner appointed physician extraordinary to King George IV

1823
Jenner dies

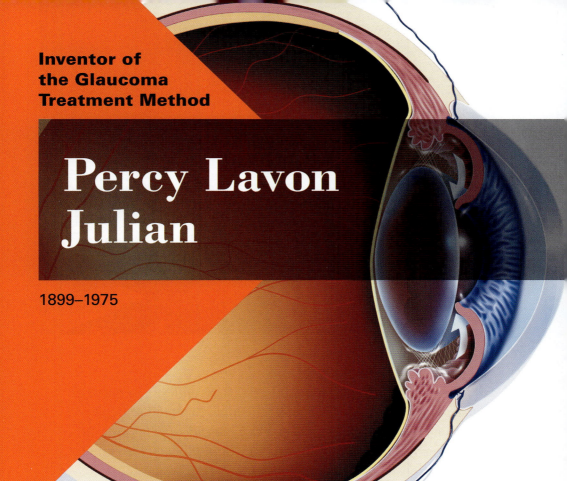

Inventor of the Glaucoma Treatment Method

Percy Lavon Julian

1899–1975

All inventors overcome barriers to make their inventions come to life. Some deal with harsh criticism from their contemporaries, while others suffer effects of different natures. Out of these struggles comes great works. The health and medical industries have benefited from inventors who overcome obstacles. Percy Lavon Julian, for instance, overcame criticism and alienation to introduce his inventions to society and change the face of medicine forever.

A Successful Youth

Percy Lavon Julian was born in Montgomery, Alabama, on April 11, 1899, the oldest of six children. His grandparents had been slaves, and his father worked as a railway mail clerk.

Dr. Percy Julian, pictured in his office in Chicago in 1947

Julian's parents strongly encouraged their children to become educated, but laws in Alabama forced Julian to attend segregated elementary schools that offered inferior education. Moreover, in Montgomery, no high school accepted black students. Instead of attending high school, Julian attended a trade school.

Although the schools Julian attended offered few science classes, he was fascinated by science and read about it on his own. He particularly liked chemistry, an interest that troubled his parents, who were concerned that racial discrimination would make it impossible for an African American to make a living as a chemist.

Julian persuaded them to let him try, however, and in 1916 he gained admission to DePauw University in Greencastle, Indiana. Since Julian had not attended an academic high school, he was required to take classes at the high school level in addition to regular college classes. He also had to work to finance his tuition. Despite these challenges, Julian graduated from DePauw in 1920 as class **valedictorian**, an achievement that so delighted his parents that they moved the family to Greencastle and sent all of Julian's siblings to DePauw.

Facing Struggle

Given his strong academic record at DePauw, Julian expected to be awarded a fellowship that would allow him to continue studying chemistry as a graduate student. Such fellowships were not forthcoming because of his race, however, so Julian took a job teaching chemistry at Fisk University, a black college in Nashville, Tennessee.

Julian's professors at DePauw kept lobbying for him. Finally, in 1922 Julian was awarded a fellowship to Harvard University in Cambridge, Massachusetts, where he studied **organic chemistry**. Julian received his master's degree in 1923 and continued to work at Harvard as a researcher for a couple of years, hoping for a permanent position.

The position did not materialize, however, so Julian left Harvard and went back to teaching, becoming the only professor of chemistry at West Virginia Collegiate Institute. In 1928, he moved to Washington, DC, to teach at Howard University, a black college.

A year later, Julian received a fellowship to study for a doctorate in organic chemistry at the University of Vienna in Austria. The opportunity was the realization of a dream and offered a chance to study under Ernst Späth (1886–1946), an extremely well-respected chemist who had been synthesizing naturally occurring chemicals in his laboratory.

Julian received his doctorate in 1931 and returned to Howard. A dispute with the administration led him to leave Howard a year later and take a research position at DePauw. There, he and a colleague developed a method to synthesize a drug to treat glaucoma, an eye disease.

> "My dear friends, who daily climb uncertain hills in the countries of their minds, hills that have to do with the future of our country and of our children, may I humbly submit to you, the only thing that has enabled me to keep doing the creative work, was the constant determination: Take heart! Go farther on!"
> —Percy Lavon Julian

Despite Julian's success, his race still stood in the way of his professional advancement. The Institute of Paper Chemistry wanted to hire Julian, but it was located in the town of Appleton, Wisconsin, where a law forbade African Americans from staying overnight.

One day the institute's board was discussing the impossibility of hiring Julian, which was a source of great frustration to the executives. One member of the board was also an executive at Glidden Company, a paint and chemical company located in Chicago. Glidden used soybeans to make some of its products and wanted to employ an organic chemist to help develop more lucrative products. As Chicago had no laws forbidding African Americans from residing there, the executive called Julian and offered him a job at Glidden.

Julian had wanted to be a professor at DePauw, but the university would not appoint an African American to a professorship, so he accepted the offer from Glidden. In 1936, he went to work for the company as director of research for its soybean division.

Defining the Problem

At the time, soybeans were not widely used in the United States. Julian had studied the soybean while in Vienna and knew that the bean contained a plethora of compounds. At Glidden, he developed methods to purify useful products from soybeans, including lecithin, used to keep processed foods from separating, and soybean meal, an important source of protein in animal feed. He also developed a fire-suppressant foam made from soybean protein that was widely used by the US Navy during World War II to fight fires on ships.

What really interested Julian about soybeans was their chemical compounds, which are very similar to human hormones. Julian thought it might be possible to make human hormones from soy compounds, but the process used to extract the compounds from soy oil destroyed the valuable oil.

A break came one day in 1940, when water leaked into a tank containing soy oil, creating a white mass. Julian tested the mass and discovered that it contained large amounts of the hormone-like soy compounds. The oil had not been ruined, so Julian developed a separation process based on what had happened during the leak.

Glaucoma Treatment

At DePauw in the 1930s, Julian and Joseph Pikl, a colleague he had worked with in Vienna, began working on synthesizing the organic chemical physostigmine, which occurs naturally in small quantities in the West African Calabar bean. Physostigmine had been shown to be an effective treatment for some forms of glaucoma, a disease in which pressure builds up in the eye, eventually causing blindness.

Extracting enough physostigmine from Calabar beans to create a useful dose of medicine was an expensive and difficult process. Julian and Pikl went to work trying to synthesize physostigmine more cheaply in the laboratory.

They were not alone in trying to synthesize the chemical: a group of British scientists led by the respected chemist Robert Robinson, who would go on to win the Nobel Prize, had also been trying to make physostigmine in the laboratory. Robinson's team thought they were very close to a solution, and most scientists assumed that Robinson would solve the physostigmine problem.

In 1935, however, Julian and Pikl published a paper showing that they had successfully created physostigmine in the laboratory. Not only had they beaten Robinson, but their paper also proved that Robinson's work was deeply in error. The reversal astounded the scientific world and gave glaucoma patients an inexpensive and reliable new source of medication to help save their sight.

The new process allowed him to obtain the soy compounds in large quantities. He then developed methods to transform the hormone-like compounds into actual human hormones. He soon created a method to cheaply synthesize the human hormone progesterone, which is used by doctors to help pregnant women avoid miscarriage.

Designing the Solution

Julian moved on to develop ways to synthesize other hormones from soy. In 1948, scientists discovered that the hormone cortisone could be an effective treatment for rheumatoid arthritis; Julian quickly began work on synthesizing cortisone.

Rheumatoid arthritis is a crippling ailment that develops when the body's immune system attacks its own joints. Cortisone suppresses the immune system, providing relief to sufferers of the disease. In addition, cortisone was also found to be effective in treating other illnesses caused by immune system malfunction. In its natural form, however, cortisone was very expensive, costing about $700 per gram, and most of those who needed it could not afford it. In late 1949, Julian developed a method to create, from the soybean, synthetic cortisone that cost only about 50 cents per gram.

Dr. Percy Julian working in his lab

Applying the Solution

Julian's work provided much-needed relief to sufferers of rheumatoid arthritis and brought him renown. At times, however, his elevated public profile made him a target for racial violence. In 1950, Julian and his family moved into the wealthy, largely white Chicago suburb of Oak Park. Before the family moved in, vandals tried to set fire to the house, and several months later the house was bombed.

The Impact of the Solution on Society

In 1953, Julian resigned from Glidden because he wanted to extend his research from soybeans to other promising plants. The following year he founded Julian Laboratories in Oak Park and began studying a wild yam found in Mexico that contained many promising hormone-like compounds. Julian developed methods to synthesize cortisone and other useful chemicals from the yam and built factories in Mexico and Guatemala to process them.

In 1961, Julian sold his business to the large pharmaceutical firm Smith, Kline, and French, his first step toward retirement. In later life, Julian was involved in a variety of nonprofit work in science education and civil rights. He was elected to the National Academy of Science in 1973; two years later, he died at the age of seventy-six.

Julian's inventions had a major impact on the world, especially in the field of medical drug development. He helped create drugs—which are still used today—that prevented people from going blind, and he introduced news ways to identify, purify, and synthesize organic compounds. Despite a challenging life, Julian proved that he would not let circumstances defeat him. His legacy lives on to this day.

Timeline

1899
Percy Julian born in Montgomery, Alabama

1920
Julian graduates from DePauw University

1931
Julian earns doctorate in organic chemistry

1936
Julian accepts position at Glidden Company

1949
Julian develops method for creating synthetic cortisone

1954
Julian founds Julian Laboratories

1973
Julian elected to the National Academy of Science

1975
Julian dies

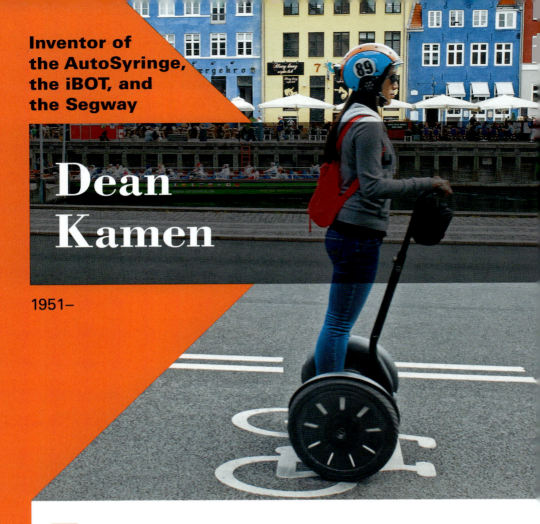

Inventor of the AutoSyringe, the iBOT, and the Segway

Dean Kamen

1951–

Throughout the history of invention, many men and women created their products in relative obscurity. They did not invent to gain celebrity status, but rather they invented because they wanted to improve the world. One such inventor is Dean Kamen, who developed lifesaving medical devices such as the AutoSyringe and the iBOT. His most famous invention, however, is the Segway scooter. Above all, Kamen works to achieve success with the products he creates.

Starting Out

Dean Kamen was born in 1951 and grew up in Rockville Centre, a town located on Long Island, New York. Kamen's father was a

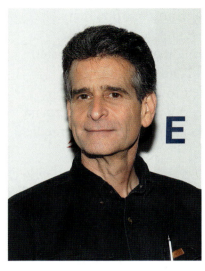

Dean Kamen

successful illustrator, and his mother was a teacher; both parents wanted their children to do well in school. His older brother Bart was an exceptional student and eventually became a physician. Dean, in contrast, found school uninteresting and restrictive. He became a discipline problem and deliberately got poor grades on tests.

During high school, Kamen began tinkering with machinery on his own. He began designing light boxes, used to create audiovisual presentations. By the time he graduated from high school, Kamen was operating a successful small business out of his parents' basement.

At his parents' insistence, Kamen went to college, attending the Worcester Polytechnic Institute in Massachusetts. Although he attended classes, he devoted much of his time—he often went home on the weekends—to his light-box business.

The First Taste of Success

While Dean Kamen attended Worcester Polytechnic, Bart Kamen attended Harvard Medical School. Bart noticed that the intravenous units used in hospitals to provide patients with fluids, nutrients, and drugs were difficult to use. The big, bulky units needed constant monitoring to ensure that they were providing patients with the correct drug dosage.

Bart suggested designing a new, automatic intravenous device to his younger brother. Intrigued by the challenge, Kamen went to work, building what would become the first drug infusion pump in 1971, when he was twenty years old. Infusion pumps administer medications directly into patients' circulatory systems. The prestigious *New England Journal of Medicine* did a story on the pump, and Kamen was flooded with inquiries.

Work on the pump took up so much of Kamen's time that he dropped out of college. In 1976, he started a new company, AutoSyringe, Inc., and began manufacturing the pumps. Frustrated by New York's high taxes, Kamen moved AutoSyringe to New Hampshire in 1979. AutoSyringe continued to grow, and Kamen eventually decided that he did not want to run a large manufacturing company. In 1982, he sold the company to the large drug and medical-device company Baxter International.

With the money he received from the sale of AutoSyringe, Kamen decided to start his own research and development company. Kamen combined the first two letters of his first and last names to form the company's name, DEKA Research and Development Corp. DEKA

FIRST

Kamen's own experience in school was far from ideal; despite his strong interest in science and engineering, he found his science and math classes dull. As he grew older, Kamen began to see his experience as symptomatic of a larger problem: although science can be very exciting, it is often not presented as such to young people. To Kamen, this attitude toward science is wrongheaded and potentially very harmful. He knows that the vast majority of people will never be talented and lucky enough to become stars in sports, movies, or music, but that many of them could be productive scientists. Kamen argues that the economic future of the United States depends on technological advancement and that because of the current lack of glamour surrounding science, fewer young people go into the field, and so there are fewer inventions and advances.

To help young people see the value of pursuing science, Kamen created a nonprofit organization, FIRST (For Inspiration and Recognition of Science and Technology), in 1989. FIRST hosts a robotics competition in which teams of high school students design and build robots to perform certain tasks, which change from year to year.

was located in Manchester, New Hampshire, where it created new devices and sold the rights to manufacture them to other companies.

In 1987, Baxter asked DEKA to improve its dialysis machine. A dialysis machine cleans waste products from the blood so that they do not poison the body, a function normally performed by the kidneys.

Existing dialysis machines were large, heavy, noisy, expensive, and difficult to operate and maintain. As a result, the machines were usually located only in hospitals or clinics and could not be used at home by patients suffering from kidney failure. Additionally, some patients needed dialysis as often as twice a week, and the process took several hours.

Kamen and his staff dramatically redesigned the dialysis machine. Their machine, which went on the market in 1993, weighed less than 25 pounds (11 kg), was relatively cheap, and was fairly simple

FIRST has expanded greatly since its inception and has added a competition using robots made of Legos for younger students, as well as a tech challenge competition. As of 2014, FIRST has reached over four hundred thousand students with its many programs.

Former presidential candidate Jon Huntsman (*upper right*) operates a remote-control robot at the FIRST summer school.

Dean Kamen

to operate. Thus individuals could run it at home. The machine was also very quiet—patients were able to undergo dialysis while they slept. The new machine made life far easier for people suffering from kidney failure—some could work and even travel.

Defining the Problem

One day in the late 1980s, Kamen was walking down the street when he saw a man in a wheelchair struggling to get the chair over a curb. The man then went into an ice cream store, where he had to struggle again to reach across the counter to make his purchase.

Kamen was bothered by the shortcomings of the wheelchair. The wheelchair was supposed to make getting around easier for people with physical limitations, yet a curb posed a serious obstacle. Additionally, wheelchairs restricted people to a low sitting position, and many counters and cabinets were designed for people who could stand. Moreover, wheelchairs were likely to tip over. In the early 1990s, Kamen decided to create a more mobile, stable wheelchair.

Designing the Solution

In 2000, Kamen's improved wheelchair, the iBOT, which featured an elaborate balancing system, came onto the market. The system used gyroscopes to detect instability. When instability was detected, a computerized system in the chair repositioned the wheels to make the chair stable again.

The iBOT balanced so well that it could operate on only two wheels. The chair had a four-wheel base that could tip upright so that only two wheels were touching the ground; this ability also made the chair taller, to allow a user to reach high counters and interact more easily with people who were standing. The base could also flip over, enabling it to climb stairs.

Applying the Solution

Kamen sold the rights to the iBOT—nicknamed Fred after the dancer Fred Astaire—to Johnson & Johnson but remained convinced that his balancing technology could be adapted for a day-to-day transportation device. He reserved the right to use the system in nonmedical devices. In 1998, DEKA's staff went to work on the new transportation device.

The new device was called Ginger, after Fred Astaire's dance partner, Ginger Rogers. Ginger also used the iBOT's sophisticated balancing technology but needed only two wheels. A rider would stand on a platform between the wheels, steering with a handlebar that extended up from the wheelbase. Ginger was very responsive to cues from a rider and could travel up to 12 miles per hour (19 kmh).

Kamen was so confident about the technology used in Ginger that he decided to handle the device's manufacturing himself, rather than selling the rights to another company. He asked a journalist, Steve Kemper, to chronicle the development of what he felt sure would be an invention of great historic significance.

> "You have teenagers thinking they're going to make millions as NBA stars when that's not realistic for even 1 percent of them. Becoming a scientist or engineer is."
> —Dean Kamen

Kamen needed outside funding to develop and manufacture Ginger on a large scale, so he began showing it to various investors and technology luminaries including Steve Jobs of Apple Computer and Jeffrey Bezos of Amazon.com.

Kemper wanted to write a book about Ginger, so his agent submitted proposals to various publishers. The proposal's description of Ginger was left intentionally mysterious to prevent other writers from stealing the idea for the book, but it included praise from Jobs and Bezos.

In January 2001, the proposal was leaked to a website; its appearance on the web led to a flurry of online speculation about the nature of Ginger. Fanned by Kamen's renown as an inventor, the speculation spread to the mainstream news media, creating a frenzy; it was even suggested that Ginger could be a hovercraft or a device powered by hydrogen.

Although Kamen released statements calling some of the speculation "beyond whimsical," he had overestimated his invention's appeal. Kamen claimed, and apparently genuinely believed, that

Ginger would revolutionize American society, altering the way cities were built in much the way the automobile had done.

On December 3, 2001, Kamen unveiled Ginger—now called the Segway—on the television show *Good Morning America*. The response of one of the show's hosts, Diane Sawyer, reflected the disappointment felt by many; she said, "But that can't be it." The Segway became available in 2003 to consumers at a cost of almost $5,000. Although sales numbers have never been released, the Segway was not a popular success.

The Segway had no chance of living up to some people's expectations, but hype was not the only problem. Kamen had developed a technology that was very interesting from an engineering point of view but not as interesting to consumers. Throughout its development, Kamen had insisted that the Segway not be called a scooter. To the average consumer, however, that is exactly what the Segway is. The fact that it has an advanced balancing and steering system makes very little difference to someone who does not want a scooter in the first place. Dialysis machines and wheelchairs have a captive market; a scooter is physically necessary to almost no one, so better ones are not desperately needed.

The Impact of the Solution on Society

Although enthusiasm for the Segway appears to have died down, Kamen has benefited from the publicity he received during the run-up to its unveiling. The publicity generated interest in his other projects, among them the FIRST robotics competitions. Other products have impacted society, too. In 2014, Kamen introduced a new generator, called the Beacon 10, to the market. The Beacon 10 is an improvement of an earlier generator, called the Stirling engine. It could be used to bring electricity to poorer, rural parts of the world.

One of the fields he is most passionate about is prosthetics. He and his team have spent months developing more advanced prosthetic limbs that offer people—especially wounded soldiers—new ways to interact with the world around them. For his work as a prolific inventor, Kamen received the National Medal of Technology in 2000, the Lemelson-MIT Prize in 2002, and the American Society of Mechanical Engineering Medal in 2007.

Kamen is a man of many talents whose inventions have revolutionized the industries for which they were intended. His influence on aspiring scientists and inventors is well known, and his dedication to new and more efficient technologies has brought him fame and a place in history books.

Timeline

1951
Kamen born; grows up in Rockville Centre, Long Island

1971
Kamen builds the first drug infusion pump

1976
Kamen founds AutoSyringe, Inc.

1982
Kamen sells AutoSyringe to Baxter International

1987
Kamen's new company, DEKA, works on improved dialysis machine

1993
Kamen's dialysis machine goes on the market

1998
DEKA begins work on a secret new transportation project

2000
Kamen's iBOT wheelchair becomes available

2001
Amid widespread speculation, Kamen introduces his new invention, the Segway

Pioneer in Anesthesia Device

William Morton

1819–1868

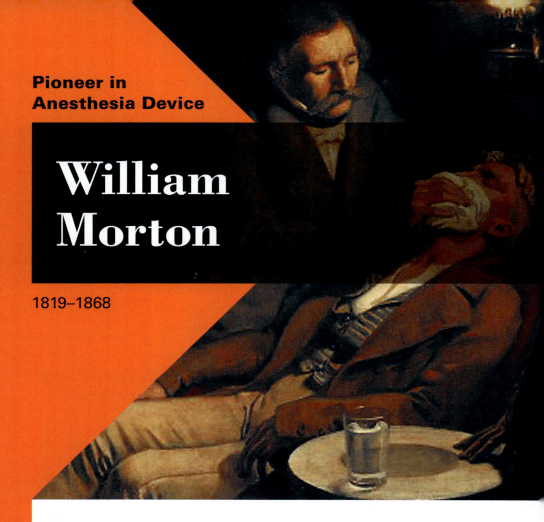

The medical industry has evolved time and time again, with new inventions creating new opportunities for better products that benefit humanity. Since early human history, evidence of surgeries being performed has survived. This information, along with written documents of surgeries later on, was used to conduct surgeries and improve upon them. Until the nineteenth century, patients were fully conscious during all surgical procedures. Then, one inventor, William Morton, developed a device that could safely deliver gas called ether to patients and put them to sleep. This device changed the way surgeries were performed and led to preserving the lives of many patients.

Youth

Portrait of William T. G. Morton

William Thomas Green Morton was born on August 19, 1819, in Charlton, Massachusetts, to James Morton, a farmer, and his wife, Rebecca. At the age of seventeen William Morton went to Boston, where he worked as a clerk and salesman. Hoping to embark on a more satisfying and lucrative career, in 1840 he moved to Baltimore, Maryland, to study dentistry. He did not complete a degree but went on to become a pupil of Horace Wells, a dentist in Hartford, Connecticut. In the winter of 1842, Morton and Wells established a dental practice together in Boston. However, the business failed to make money, and the partnership was dissolved on friendly terms in the fall of 1843.

In March 1844, Morton enrolled at the Harvard Medical School with the aim of completing his medical training. His chemistry professor, Charles T. Jackson, encouraged Morton's growing interest in **anesthesia**. Morton's marriage to Elizabeth Whitman in 1844, however, imposed new financial demands, leading Morton to abandon his studies and return to practicing dentistry to earn a living.

Defining the Problem

At the time, pain was a fundamental problem in surgical and dental procedures, and Morton was not alone in trying to find a solution. Many of his nineteenth-century contemporaries were interested in anesthetic gases, such as chloroform, and techniques for administering them. Scientific lecturers demonstrated the effects of nitrous oxide (often called laughing gas), using audience members as test subjects, often to comic effect. Elijah Pope, a dentist, and Crawford Williamson Long, a physician, had both used ether as an anesthetic in 1842, but neither man had publicized his results. Morton's former mentor, Horace Wells, was using nitrous oxide as a dental anesthetic by 1844, but his public demonstration of a tooth extraction under anesthesia, at which Morton assisted, turned to disaster when the bag containing the gas was inadvertently removed too soon, and the patient cried out in pain. Wells was denounced as a fraud and his career was ruined.

Morton first became interested in anesthesia around 1841, when he needed a pain-free way to extract the roots of old teeth in patients he was fitting with artificial teeth. He tried stimulants, champagne, opium, and mesmerism (a form of hypnotism), none of which proved satisfactory. In Charles Jackson's laboratory at Harvard, Morton had become familiar with the anesthetic properties of sulfuric ether gas and gradually, most likely after consulting with Jackson, Morton began to experiment with the substance on goldfish, a hen, the family

Anesthesia Today

General anesthesia, in which the patient is rendered unconscious during surgery, works quite differently from local anesthesia, in which a limited area of the body is deadened to sensation, as in the numbing of nerves in the mouth using Novocain during dental procedures. In local anesthesia, the molecules of anesthetic agents bind specifically on certain proteins in neurons near the injection site, restricting nerve blocks to a local area. Consequently, local anesthetics do not affect the brain. General anesthetic compounds, by contrast, affect the entire brain, although scientists still do not understand precisely how they work.

Ether and chloroform, popular inhalation anesthetics during the nineteenth century, are now obsolete and have been replaced by newer inhalation agents such as halothane, enflurane, isoflurane, desflurane, and sevoflurane. Nitrous oxide, however, is still in use.

Inhalation anesthetics are administered through a face mask, using an apparatus that is similar in concept to Morton's letheon, but vastly dog, and, eventually, himself. At last satisfied that the substance was safe, Morton successfully pulled the tooth of an anesthetized patient on September 30, 1846.

Morton's landmark public demonstration of ether anesthesia took place on October 16, 1846, at the Massachusetts General Hospital in Boston. Before a live audience, Morton used an inhaler device to administer a gas he mysteriously called letheon after Lethe, the river in Greek mythology whose waters induced forgetfulness. In fact, the gas was just sulfuric ether, to which Morton had added opium and aromatic oils. Prominent surgeon John Collins Warren then successfully removed a tumor from the neck of the etherized patient, a young man named Gilbert Abbott.

Designing the Solution

Morton's letheon inhaler consisted of a glass jar attached to a hose that connected to a mouthpiece designed to fit snugly over the patient's face. A sponge saturated with ether was placed inside the

more sophisticated. Standard modern practice is to use **intravenous** anesthetic agents in combination with inhalational anesthetics. The goal is to induce loss of consciousness, loss of sensation, **amnesia**, suppression of reflex reactions, and relaxation of the muscles. No single drug, however, can accomplish all of these effects.

Inhalation anesthetics are largely insoluble (unable to be dissolved) in blood or water but highly soluble in lipids (fat molecules). This characteristic of inhalation anesthetics is the basis for one theory of how the agents work: the lipid theory. Gas molecules travel through the lungs and blood to the brain, which contains an abundance of lipid-like membranes and lipid-like hydrophobic (water-free) pockets in some of its proteins. The gas molecules clearly affect specific regions of the brain, but the exact molecular mechanism remains a mystery. This problem is a very exciting area for further research because a better understanding of how anesthesia works may provide insights into consciousness itself.

glass container, and the gas released from the sponge flowed through the hose to the mouthpiece, to be inhaled by the patient.

Almost immediately, Morton applied for a patent to protect his rights to his invention. He did not reveal that the active ingredient in his letheon was ether. This lack of full disclosure, along with Morton's desire to profit from his invention, subsequently brought the dentist some criticism. Morton stated, however, that he was prepared to grant licenses for the use of his apparatus and discovery, and he authorized certain charitable hospitals to use the technology free of charge. Morton also obtained a patent in England. By the end of 1846, operations had been performed using ether anesthesia in London and Paris.

Applying the Solution

Controversy quickly erupted over the real originator of ether anesthesia. Jackson, in particular, claimed credit. The French Academy of Science investigated and decided to offer a prize of 5,000 francs to Morton and Jackson jointly, but Morton refused his half of the money, insisting that he deserved sole credit. Complicated legal disputes ensued with other parties, notably Horace Wells and Crawford Long. Morton on several occasions petitioned Congress for compensation, without success.

During the Civil War, the use of ether allowed thousands of soldiers to endure amputation with the crucial help of anesthesia. Several plans were proposed to give Morton financial support, but none materialized.

When Morton died in New York in 1868, at the age of forty-eight, his finances and energies had been seriously depleted by his legal battle. In spite of the controversies that beset him, Morton made a significant contribution to anesthesiology through his experiments and by being the first to demonstrate anesthesia to the medical community at large.

The Impact of the Solution on Society

The discovery of ether anesthesia was an essential step in the development of modern surgery. After Morton's time, general anesthesia became increasingly popular, but it remained an imperfect science until well into the twentieth century. Patients often died because of overdoses or breathing difficulties. In the aftermath of the attack on Pearl Harbor in 1941, it was discovered that anesthetic doses that were well tolerated by healthy people could kill individuals who were in shock from loss of blood.

Still, with advancements from people like Morton, medicine as a science became more refined and easier to navigate and improve upon. Likewise, it led to fewer deaths. Without Morton and men and women like him, surgery today might be just as it was centuries ago. Morton's advancements in particular propelled the medical industry into a new direction, where painless surgery was possible and not just a myth.

Timeline

1819
William Morton born in Charlton, Massachusetts

1840
Morton goes to Baltimore to study dentistry

1842
Morton returns to Boston and begins practicing dentistry

1844
Morton briefly studies medicine at Harvard University

1846
Morton performs a tooth extraction under general ether anesthesia

1849–1854
Other parties dispute Morton's claims to right of discovery of anesthesia

1868
Morton dies in New York City

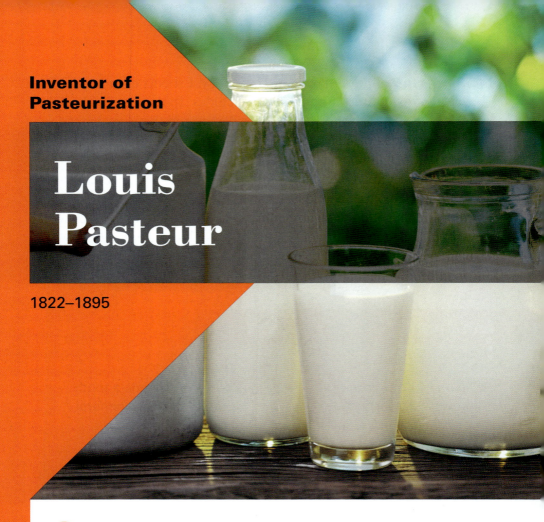

Inventor of Pasteurization

Louis Pasteur

1822–1895

Some inventors create inventions for more than one industry. These people apply their knowledge and creativity to transforming industries for the better. One such inventor is Louis Pasteur. His inventions benefited not only the medical industry but also the food industry. Pasteur is one of the most well-known inventors of the nineteenth century. His process (later named pasteurization, after him) of preserving milk and other foods challenged existing preservation concepts of the time. Likewise, he was the first person to prove that germs caused disease, and his invention of multiple vaccines helped save the lives of many people.

Louis Pasteur

Birth of an Inventor

One of the nineteenth century's most distinguished scientists, Louis Pasteur was born on December 27, 1822. He was the son of a tanner and spent his childhood in the small French town of Arbois. Science held little interest for him as a boy; his passion was painting and drawing—he made pastel portraits of his family and friends and dreamed of becoming an artist or art professor.

Although he worked hard, his teachers did not find him especially gifted. At age seventeen, he received his bachelor's of arts degree at the Royal College in the town of Besançon; this was followed by his bachelor's of science two years later. At that time, he planned to become a teacher and attended the École Normale Supérieure, a teacher training college in Paris, the French capital. There he earned two additional degrees: a master's of science in 1845 and a doctorate in chemistry in 1847.

Early Experiments

In the late 1840s, Pasteur made his first important discovery—he was studying tartaric acid, a substance that forms when grapes ferment and produce alcohol. Pasteur began testing how crystals of the acid behaved when he shone different kinds of light onto and into them. He tried using **polarized light** and discovered that some forms of the acid made polarized light rays bend one way, whereas other forms made the light rays bend in the opposite direction. He realized that the molecules of certain substances, such as tartaric acid, can exist in two different forms (called stereoisomers) that are mirror images of each other, like a person's two hands.

At the age of twenty-six, Pasteur announced this important finding to the world on May 22, 1848, by reading his research paper to the Paris Academy of Sciences. His brilliant discovery earned him a job as a professor of chemistry at the University of Strasbourg.

Defining the Problem

A few years later, in 1854, Pasteur had moved to the University of Lille in southern France to work with a faculty established to solve industrial problems. While there, he was asked to help brewers discover why wines turn bad. He began to look closely at the process of **fermentation**, which was then poorly understood. Looking through his microscope, Pasteur found that yeast, used in brewing, contains living bacteria. Some of these bacteria are essential for brewing—fermentation cannot happen without them. Others, however, make the wine or beer turn bad after it has fermented.

Designing the Solution

Pasteur's solution to the problem was simple. After a batch of wine had fermented, he proposed heating it to around 122 degrees Fahrenheit (50 degrees Celsius) to kill most of the remaining bacteria. When the wine cooled, it would have fewer microorganisms to turn it sour and it would keep longer. This process became known as pasteurization and was soon being used to preserve milk, beer, vinegar, and other food products.

Applying the Solution

The development of pasteurization demonstrated that great benefits could result from linking science and industry. Pasteur firmly believed in this connection and championed anything that broke down the barriers between scientists and the ordinary community. He put his convictions into practice at the University of Lille in the 1850s. Recognizing the need to take scientific ideas into the community, he began teaching evening classes to young factory workers from the area. His interest in education continued in the 1860s when he was made administrator and director of scientific studies at the École des Beaux-Arts in Paris. From that time on, he combined his teaching work with scientific research.

Studying Germs

Pasteur's work on fermentation led him into a broader study of germs and their origin. Around this time, many scientists believed in the idea of spontaneous generation: they thought that germs could arise from anything—for example, dirt. Pasteur refused to accept this belief. Having seen that bacteria caused wine and milk to go bad, he believed germs were living organisms carried through the air. Thus, if germs were prevented from traveling, they could not spread disease. His hypothesis, called the germ theory, had gradually been developed by other scientists, including John Snow (1813–1858) and Robert Koch (1843–1910). However, no one had conclusively proved that the theory was correct. Pasteur devised a laboratory experiment to prove that germs travel through the air. He put some broth in a sealed container with a U-shaped tube at the top. He found that the U-tube prevented bacteria from entering. When the broth did not develop mold, as it would normally have done, this helped to prove that germs are carried in the air.

> "In the fields of observation, chance favors only the prepared mind."
> —Louis Pasteur

Germs, in Pasteur's view, not only made food go bad, they also carried diseases between humans. Those who believed in spontaneous generation refused to accept this: how could a microscopic organism kill a much larger living creature? In the mid-1860s, Pasteur had an opportunity to prove he was right when the French government asked him to help its silk industry, which was then in crisis. Silk farmers were in despair because a disease had killed many of their silkworms and dramatically reduced production. After three years of research, Pasteur found that the disease was caused by a tiny microorganism that infects silkworm eggs. He showed that destroying infected eggs and selecting disease-free ones could eradicate the disease. This work, and his previous work on fermentation, helped to prove what became known as the germ theory of disease—the idea that diseases are spread by germs and do not arise spontaneously.

Soon after this triumph, Pasteur suffered a stroke and was left partly paralyzed. He spent months in bed recovering, and it was unclear for some time whether he would ever work again. His health remained poor, and he walked with a limp for the rest of his life. Working as administrator at the École des Beaux-Arts was now too arduous, and he applied for retirement from teaching. Recognizing his enormous contribution to French industry, the French emperor, Napoleon III, and the parliament of France set up a personal laboratory for him in Paris where he could continue his work.

With the germ theory now established, Pasteur was able to take practical steps to prevent diseases—but his next breakthrough came by accident. He had been planning to infect chickens with the bacteria that would give them cholera, to study how that disease occurred. He and his assistant, Charles Chamberland (1851–1908), went on vacation and forgot about the cholera bacteria for an entire month. Later, when they tried to infect the chickens with this old, weak batch of bacteria, the chickens became unwell but did not die. Furthermore,

Pasteurization

To discover why wine and beer went bad over time, Louis Pasteur investigated the fermentation process, which uses bacteria to turn sugar into alcohol in an anaerobic (oxygen-free) environment. "In short," Pasteur wrote, "fermentation is a very general phenomenon. It is life without air, or life without free oxygen." The bacteria enabling fermentation, however, were accompanied by other bacteria that were harmful to humans if ingested. In response, Pasteur developed the process of pasteurization, a way of killing most of the harmful bacteria inside food. In the modern world, pasteurization is most familiar as a way of preserving milk, although it can also be used to prolong the life of many other foods, including beer, wine, fruit juice, eggs, cheese, honey, and canned foods.

Pasteurization resembles cooking. One reason for cooking food is to make it safe to eat: raising food to a high temperature for a certain length of time destroys the harmful bacteria inside it. Not all foods can be cooked, however. People like to eat food such as dairy products and consume drinks such as wine and beer uncooked;

Pasteur discovered that afterward, he could not infect those chickens with a new, more powerful batch of the bacteria. He realized that the original, weak bacteria had made the chickens immune: quite by accident, he had developed a vaccine to prevent chicken cholera.

Pasteur applied the same thinking to other diseases, including anthrax, a sheep and cattle disease that can also kill humans, and rabies, a fatal disease that is spread by bites from infected animals or contact with their saliva. In the 1870s, when Pasteur announced he had produced an anthrax vaccine, his fellow scientists greeted the news with disbelief, so Pasteur agreed to a public test. He put forty-eight sheep into a field and inoculated half of them with his vaccine, which was a weak form of anthrax. He left the other sheep untreated. Later, he infected all the sheep with a more powerful form of anthrax. Within days, the twenty-four unvaccinated sheep were dead; the others remained healthy. The anthrax issue remained controversial, however. Later, it was discovered that Pasteur had used not his own

---

foods like these cannot be cooked in the same way as meat or fish without changing their flavor or appearance greatly. Pasteurization helps to solve these problems by "cooking" the foods long enough to kill harmful bacteria but not long enough to change their taste unacceptably.

Until the invention of pasteurization, many foods and drinks could be kept in their raw state only a short time before they went bad. When people lived in smaller, more geographically constrained communities, they usually bought perishables daily from a local seller. In the modern world, however, food products are often prepared days or weeks ahead of sale, and they may be transported considerable distances from where they are manufactured to the grocery stores where people buy them. That brings great economic benefits to food manufacturers, who can ship food products farther, and to stores, which can keep them on the shelves longer. It also helps consumers, who can buy food products far ahead of the time that they plan to consume them.

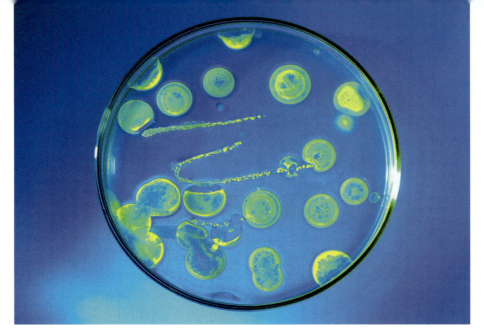

Bacteria (in green) grows on a petri dish.

vaccine but one originally developed by French veterinarian Jean-Joseph-Henri Toussaint.

During the following decade, Pasteur successfully produced a vaccine for rabies from the tissues of animals that had died of the disease. Using this treatment, he claimed to have vaccinated a dog against rabies with a course of fourteen injections. On July 6, 1885, Pasteur used this vaccine to treat a young boy, Joseph Meister, who had been bitten by a rabid dog. Although Pasteur was initially reluctant to use his vaccine on a human, he realized that the boy would certainly die without treatment and finally agreed. After a number of injections, the boy was cured—and Pasteur earned great public acclaim. The vaccine caused some scientific debate during the following years, however. Some physicians argued that it was not nearly as effective as Pasteur claimed, and others suggested that Pasteur put people at great risk by allowing his vaccine to be used before it had been properly tested.

Whatever the truth of the matter, the public success of the rabies vaccine led to the final triumph of Pasteur's career. In 1888, in honor of Pasteur, many French people donated money to establish a laboratory where scientists could research the prevention and treatment of disease. It was named the Pasteur Institute; Louis Pasteur served as its director until he died on September 28, 1895. A lasting tribute to one of France's greatest national heroes, the laboratory continues to be one of the world's most important institutions for the study of disease.

The Impact of the Solution on Society

Pasteur never forgot that science has important real-world applications. His work helping the French food and clothing industries and his development of medical vaccines brought important economic benefits and saved many lives. His work also marked the beginning of an age when scientists began to understand the causes of disease. The germ theory was especially important because it gave physicians a practical way to approach the treatment of diseases such as anthrax as well as an understanding of how those diseases were transmitted.

Although Pasteur is considered a scientific hero, his work was controversial during his lifetime and remains so today. In the 1880s, Robert Koch, a German physician who made many important advances in the study of bacteria, bitterly attacked his French rival: "Pasteur deserves criticism not only for his defective methods, but also for the way in which he has publicized his investigations." Koch claimed that Pasteur was too secretive about his methods, so others could not confirm his results, and charged that Pasteur was more of a showman than a scientist: "In science, facts are decisive; beautiful and well-constructed speech is not." Pasteur replied to Koch's charges in detail, ending his letter: "Entirely violent as are your attacks, Monsieur, they will not impede [the progress of my work]."

Koch was not alone. Pasteur's research often owed more to the work of others than he acknowledged. The germ theory, for example, was originally developed by others; however, Pasteur's experiments played a crucial role in proving that it was correct. Pasteur was also accused of stealing his famous anthrax vaccine from Jean-Joseph-Henri Toussaint—or, at the very least, not giving Toussaint credit. Critics also charged that Pasteur incorrectly reported his results on rabies. When his laboratory notebooks finally came to light in the late twentieth century, they seemed to show that his experiments were not as successful as he had claimed at the time. Historians have argued that Pasteur deliberately manipulated his results, perhaps because he felt under pressure to make medical breakthroughs so he could live up to his reputation.

Regardless, Pasteur's importance to the medical and the food industries cannot be denied. His place as an innovator likewise remains. He is one of the great scientists of the nineteenth century, and unlike some inventors who take advantage of success, Pasteur lived a simple life, teaching and researching despite his growing popularity. Today, much of the scientific community still regards Pasteur as an important addition to the history of society.

Timeline

1822
Louis Pasteur born; spends childhood in Arbois, France

1845
Pasteur earns master's of science at the École Normale Supérieure in Paris

1847
Pasteur earns a doctorate in chemistry

1848
Pasteur presents a paper on tartaric acid to the Paris Academy of Sciences

1854
Pasteur begins studying fermentation and develops the pasteurization process

1860s
Pasteur discovers how to eradicate pebrine

1870s
Pasteur produces an anthrax vaccine

1885
Pasteur treats a young boy with rabies

1888
Pasteur Institute is established

1895
Pasteur dies

Glossary

amnesia Absence of memory.

anesthesia A surgical gas that is inhaled by a patient to make him or her unconscious during a procedure.

arbitrator A person chosen to settle differences between two parties in controversy.

arrhythmia Differences in rhythm of the heart, either by force or nature.

compound microscope A microscope with several lenses.

cowpox A disease similar to smallpox that exists in cows and can transfer to humans.

creationist A person who does not believe in evolution.

cultivate To nurture or raise.

differentiation The sum of the processes whereby apparently indifferent cells, tissues, and structures attain their adult form and function.

electrogasdynamics The study of the behavior of electrically charged gas particles, or ions, when gas is in motion.

embryo An egg that has been fertilized and is in the process of developing.

fallopian tubes Organs that carry the egg from the ovary to the uterus.

fermentation A chemical change in which sugar turns to alcohol.

fledgling Young bird just learning to fly.

forensic science The study of crime scenes.

glaucoma An eye disease where pressure builds in the eye and gradually leads to blindness.

intravenous Describes a method of sedation where medication is fed through a plastic tube called an IV.

kinetic energy The energy of motion.

nascent Having recently come into existence.

nephrology The study of kidneys.

Nobel Prize A prize awarded every year to people who display exemplary achievement in literature, physics, chemistry, medicine, economics, or peace. It is named in honor of Alfred Nobel, a Swedish scientist.

Glossary

noxious Harmful or destructive.

nuclear DNA DNA contained within the nucleus of an organism.

organic chemistry The chemistry of carbon compounds, the basis of living things.

pasteurization A way of preserving foods by heating them briefly to kill germs.

physical therapist A person skilled in the methods of physical therapy and qualified to use these methods in the treatment of disease or disability.

polarized light Light that is filtered, like sunlight passing through polarizing sunglasses.

radioactivity High-energy rays or tiny particles given off by unstable atoms.

stethoscope An instrument that helps a physician listen to sounds inside a person's chest.

telemedicine A type of medical delivery service that uses technology to send supplies and medical treatments to remote areas of the world.

transfusion The process of taking blood from a healthy person and giving it to another who is sick or injured.

vaccination A treatment in which people are given a minute dose of the virus that causes a serious disease to prevent them from catching it later.

valedictorian A position held normally by a student who has the top grades in his or her class.

Further Information

Introduction

Books — Bryant, Jill. *Medical Inventions: The Best of Health.* Inventions That Shaped the Modern World. New York: Crabtree Publishing Company, 2013.

Nuland, Sherwin B. *Doctors: The Illustrated History of Medical Pioneers.* New York: Black Dog & Leventhal Publishers, 2008.

Websites — **Big 100: Medicine**
www.sciencechannel.com/famous-scientists-discoveries/big-100-medicine.htm

Virtual Knee Surgery
www.edheads.org/activities/knee

Patricia Bath: Inventor of Laser Cataract Surgery

Book — Braun, Sandra. *Incredible Women Inventors.* Women's Hall of Fame. Toronto: Second Story Press, 2007.

Websites — **Lemelson–MIT Program: Patricia Bath Feature**
lemelson.mit.edu/resources/patricia-bath

Women's History Month: Patricia Bath Biography
www.youtube.com/watch?v=cV7PZ9RvhLE

Bessie Blount: Inventor of Self-Feeding Apparatus for the Disabled

Book — Sullivan, Otha Richard. *Black Stars: African American Women Scientists and Inventors.* New York: Wiley, 2002.

Website — **Black American History: Bessie Blount Griffin**
blackinhistory.tumblr.com/post/51761929195/bessie-blount-griffin#.VICPht7qKJU

Herbert Boyer and Stanley Norman Cohen: Inventors of DNA Cloning

Books — Schultz, Mark. *The Stuff of Life: A Graphic Guide to Genetics and DNA.* New York: Hill and Wang, 2009.

Venter, J. Craig. *Life at the Speed of Light: From the Double Helix to the Dawn of Digital Life.* New York: Viking, 2013.

Warren, Rebecca, ed. *Timelines of Science.* New York: DK Publishing, 2013.

Further Information

Websites **CrashCourse: DNA Structure and Replication**
www.youtube.com/watch?v=8kK2zwjRV0M

What Is DNA and How Does It Work?
www.youtube.com/watch?v=zwibgNGe4aY

Keith Campbell and Ian Wilmut: Inventors of Cloning Technology

Books Dunn, Joeming. *Dolly: The First Cloned Sheep.* Famous Firsts: Animals Making History. Edina, MN: Magic Wagon, 2011.

Langwith, Jacqueline. *Cloning. Opposing Viewpoints.* Farmington Hills, MI: Greenhaven Press, 2012.

Schafer, Susan. *Cloning.* Genetics: The Science of Life. New York: Routledge, 2014.

Websites **Discovery: Human Cloning**
www.youtube.com/watch?v=7tbxN5uwaqA

The New York Times Retro Report: The Story of Dolly the Cloned Sheep
www.youtube.com/watch?v=tELZEPcgKkE

Allan Cormack and Godfrey Hounsfield: Inventors of the CT Scanner

Books Bates, Stephen, Liz Beckmann, Adrian Thomas, and Richard Waltham. *Godfrey Hounsfield: Intuitive Genius of CT.* London: The British Institute of Radiology, 2012.

Vaughan, Christopher L. *Imagining the Elephant: A Biography of Allan MacLeod Cormack.* London: Imperial College Press, 2008.

Websites **Brought to Life: CT/CAT Scanner**
www.sciencemuseum.org.uk/broughttolife/techniques/ctcatscanner.aspx

CT Scanner: How It Works
www.youtube.com/watch?v=rN4E8Y5IoAs

Raymond Damadian: Inventor of the Magnetic Resonance Imaging Scanner

Books Brodsky, Ira S. *The History & Future of Medical Technology.* St. Louis: Telescope Books, 2010.

Damadian, Raymond. *Gifted Mind: The Dr. Raymond Damadian Story*. Green Forest, AR: Master Books, 2015.

Websites **I'm Having an MRI Scan**
www.youtube.com/watch?v=xaVGsYbEnMM

KidsHealth: Magnetic Resonance Imaging
kidshealth.org/parent/system/medical/mri.html

Charles Drew: Creator of the Blood Bank

Books Harmening, Denise M. *Modern Blood Banking and Transfusion Practices*. Philadelphia: F.A. Davis Company, 2012.

Venezia, Mike. *Charles Drew: Doctor Who Got Pumped Up to Donate Blood*. Getting to Know the World's Greatest Inventors and Scientists. Chicago: Children's Press, 2009.

Websites **American Red Cross: How to Donate Blood**
www.redcrossblood.org/donating-blood/eligibility-requirements

Red Cross: Dr. Charles R. Drew—Through the Eyes of a Daughter
www.youtube.com/watch?v=O8O3Jrh5SIU

Robert Edwards and Patrick Steptoe: Inventors of Human In Vitro Fertilization

Books Jones, Dr. Howard W., Jr. *In Vitro Fertilization Comes to America: Memoir of a Medical Breakthrough*. Williamsburg, VA: Jamestowne Bookworks, 2014.

Parker, Steve. *Kill or Cure: An Illustrated History of Medicine*. New York: DK Publishing, 2013.

Websites **35 Years of IVF**
www.youtube.com/watch?v=GZzgG0IDDyQ

Robert Edwards: Biography
www.nobelprize.org/nobel_prizes/medicine/laureates/2010/edwards-facts.html

Ashok Gadgil: Inventor of the Ultraviolet Water Purification System

Books McKay, Daniel. *How to Purify Water: How to Get Drinking Water During a Crisis*. Seattle: CreateSpace, 2012.

Further Information

Salina, Irena, ed. *Written in Water: Messages of Hope for Earth's Most Precious Resource*. Washington, DC: National Geographic, 2010.

Websites   **European Inventor Award 2011 Nominee**
www.youtube.com/watch?v=CPQ2llajySk

Success Stories: UV Waterworks
www2.lbl.gov/TT/success_stories/practical_application/uv_waterworks.html

Meredith Gourdine: Inventor of a Device for Purifying the Air

Book   Walker, Robin. *Black and Science Volume Three: African American Contributions to Science and Technology*. Seattle: Reklaw Education, 2013.

Website   **Inventors: Meredith Gourdine**
inventors.about.com/library/inventors/blgourdine.htm

Wilson Greatbatch: Inventor of the Pacemaker

Books   Greatbatch, Wilson. *The Making of the Pacemaker: Celebrating a Lifesaving Invention*. Amherst, NY: Prometheus Books, 2000.

Haven, Kendall. *100 Greatest Science Inventions of All Time*. Santa Barbara, CA: Libraries Unlimited, 2005.

Jeffrey, Kirk. *Machines in Our Hearts: The Cardiac Pacemaker, the Implantable Defibrillator, and American Health Care*. Baltimore: Johns Hopkins University Press, 2001.

Websites   **American Heart Association**
www.heart.org/HEARTORG/Conditions/Arrhythmia/PreventionTreatmentofArrhythmia/Artificial-Pacemaker_UCM_448480_Article.jsp

National Heart, Lung, and Blood Institute
www.nhlbi.nih.gov/health/health-topics/topics/pace

Robert Hooke: Inventor of Various Scientific Instruments

Books   Burgan, Michael. *Robert Hooke: Natural Philosopher and Scientific Explorer*. Signature Lives: Scientific Revolution. North Mankato, MN: Compass Point Books, 2007.

	Cooper, Michael. *Robert Hooke and the Rebuilding of London*. Stroud, Gloucestershire, England: The History Press, 2013.
	Jardine, Lisa. *The Curious Life of Robert Hooke: The Man Who Measured London*. New York: HarperCollins, 2005.
Websites	**Encyclopedia Britannica: Robert Hooke** www.britannica.com/EBchecked/topic/271280/Robert-Hooke#didnt-know
	Gresham College: Robert Hooke www.youtube.com/watch?v=nuLFsHjlEVM

Edward Jenner: Inventor of the Smallpox Vaccine

Books	Henderson, D. A., and Richard Preston. *Smallpox: The Death of a Disease*. Amherst, NY: Prometheus Books, 2009.
	Willrich, Michael. *Pox: An American History*. New York: Penguin, 2012.
Websites	**TED-Ed: How We Conquered the Deadly Smallpox Virus** www.youtube.com/watch?v=yqUFy-t4MIQ
	World Health Organization www.who.int/topics/smallpox/en

Percy Lavon Julian: Inventor of the Glaucoma Treatment Method

Books	Bracks, Lean'tin. *African American Almanac: 400 Years of Triumph*. Canton, MI: Visible Ink Press, 2011.
	Stille, Darlene R. *Percy Lavon Julian: Pioneering Chemist*. Signature Lives: Modern America. North Mankato, MN: Compass Point Books, 2009.
	Walker, Robin. *Blacks and Science Volume Three: African American Contributions to Science and Technology*. Seattle: CreateSpace, 2013.
Websites	**American Chemical Society: Percy Lavon Julian** www.acs.org/content/acs/en/education/whatischemistry/landmarks/julian.html
	Nova: Forgotten Genius of Percy Lavon Julian www.youtube.com/watch?v=DuF7ss-r-m4

Further Information

Further Information

Dean Kamen: Inventor of the AutoSyringe, the iBot, and the Segway

Books   Foege, Alec. *The Tinkerers: The Amateurs, DIYers, and Inventors Who Make America Great*. New York: Basic Books, 2013.

Wilczynski, Vince, and Stephanie Slezycki. *FIRST Robots: Aim High*. Gloucester, MA: Rockport Publishers, 2007.

Websites   **FIRST**
www.usfirst.org

TED Talk: The Emotion Behind Invention
www.ted.com/talks/dean_kamen_the_emotion_behind_invention

William Morton: Pioneer in Anesthesia Device

Books   Kennedy, Michael T. *A Brief History of Disease, Science, and Medicine*. Mission Viejo, CA: Asklepiad Press, 2009.

Nuland, Sherwin B. *Doctors: The Illustrated History of Medical Pioneers*. New York: Black Dog & Leventhal Publishers, 2008.

Websites   **PBS NewsHour: The Painful Story Behind Modern Anesthesia**
www.pbs.org/newshour/rundown/the-painful-story-behind-modern-anesthesia

Utopian Surgery
www.general-anaesthesia.com

Louis Pasteur: Inventor of Pasteurization

Books   Baines, Francesca, ed. *History Year by Year*. New York: DK Publishing, 2013.

Hunter, Nick. *Louis Pasteur. Science Biographies*. Hampshire, England: Raintree Publishing, 2014.

Zamosky, Lisa. *Louis Pasteur: Founder of Microbiology*. Mission: Science Biographies. North Mankato, MN: Compass Point Books, 2008.

Websites   **Brought to Life: Germ Theory**
www.sciencemuseum.org.uk/broughttolife/techniques/germtheory.aspx

Pasteur Institute
www.pasteur.fr/en

Index

Page numbers in **boldface** are illustrations. Entries in **boldface** are glossary terms.

air purifying system, 76, 80–82
American Institute for the Prevention of Blindness, 17, 19
anesthesia, 9, 120–125
anthrax, 8, 131, 133
artificial/synthetic materials, use of in medicine, 12
AutoSyringe, 112, 113

bacteria, 8, 26–29, 128–131, **132**, 133
Bath, Patricia, 9, 15–19, **16**
blood banks, creation of, 9, 14, 56, 59–62
Blount, Bessie, 13, 20–24
Boyer, Herbert, 13, 25–32, **26**
Brown, Louis, 63, 68–69, **69**

Campbell, Keith, 33–40, **35**
cataract surgery, 9, 15, 17–18, **18**
cells, 6–7, 36, 95
cholera, 8, 73, 130–131
cloning, **11**, 13, 33–40
of DNA, 25, 27–32
Cohen, Stanley, 13, 25–32, **26**
compound microscope, 5–7
Cormack, Allan, 10, 41–48, **42**
cowpox, 8, 99, 101–103
CT (computed tomography) scans/scanner, 10, 41, **41**, 43–48

Damadian, Raymond, 10, 49–55, **50**
DEKA, 114–115, 117

DNA, 11–13, **25**, 34–38
cloning of, 25, 27–32
Dolly the sheep, 33, 38–40
Drew, Charles, 9, 56–62, **57**
drugs, invention/creation of, 6–7, 9, 111

E. coli, 26–28, **29**
Edwards, Robert, 13, 63–70, **64**, **69**
electrogasdynamics, 78, 80
ether, 120, 122–124

fermentation, 128–129
fiber optics, 13
FIRST, 114–115, **115**, 118

Gadgil, Ashok, 14, 71–75, 72
genetics, 10–13
germ theory of disease, 8, 129–130, 133
glaucoma, treatment of, 7, 107, 109
Gourdine, Meredith, 76–82, **77**, **78**
Greatbatch, Wilson, 83–90, **84**
Great Fire of London, 94–95, **95**

Hooke, Robert, 5–7, 91–96, **92**
Hounsfield, Godfrey, 10, 41–48, **42**, 47

iBot wheelchair, 14, 112, 116–117
in vitro fertilization, 13, 63, 65–70

Jenner, Edward, 8, 97–104, **98**
Julian, Percy Lavon, 7, 105–111, **106**, **110**

Kamen, Dean, 13–14, 112–119, **113**

143

Index

Lauterbur, Paul, 53–54, **54**

medicine, history of, 5–14
microscopes, 5–8, 14, 93–95
Morton, William, 9, 120–125, **120**, **121**
MRI (magnetic resonance imaging), 10, 49, **49**, **50**, 52–55

Nobel Prize, 16, 31, 41, 46, 54, 70, 109
nuclear magnetic resonance (NMR) spectroscopy, 51–53

pacemaker, 83, **83**, 86–90, **87**
Pasteur, Louis, 8, 126–134, **127**
pasteurization, 8, 126, 128, 130–131
penicillin, 7, 9, 14
physostigmine, 7, 109

rabies, 8, 132
racial segregation, 58, 106
Red Cross, 60, **61**
Roslin Institute, 33, 34, 36–38, **39**

Segway, 14, 112, **112**, 117–118
self-feeding apparatus, 13, 20, **20**, 22–24
smallpox, 8, 97, 99–104
Steptoe, Patrick, 13, 63–70, **64**, **69**
stethoscopes, 4, 8

thermometers, 4, 7–8

UV Waterworks system, 73–75

vaccination, 4, 8, 14, 97, 99–103, 126, 131–133
viruses, 8, 27, 99, 101

water purification system, ultraviolet, 14, 71, 73–75
Wilmut, Ian, 33–40, **35**
World Health Organization, 14, 103, **103**

X-rays, 4, 10, 14, 43–44